# The Ultimate 80's Kid

Anthony Lombardi

Mitt Madd Publishing—Murfreesboro, TN
ISBN: 979-8-218-33497-0
Library of Congress Control Number: 2023924092
Title: *The Ultimate 80s Kid*
Author: Anthony Lombardi
Digital distribution | 2024
Paperback | 2024

# Dedication

I would like to thank the three most important women in my life…mom, sister and wife.

My mom who always gave me words of encouragement, unconditional love and the big momma hugs and kisses. My sister for always being there for guidance and support and most importantly to my wife who is my puzzle piece and is the source of every inspiration I have.

To my incredible children, Dogboy and Sweet P, I love you so much and I am thankful every day I get to see your smiling face and give you a hug.

To my dad, my brothers, cousins and friends who helped inspire the book.

To the IHOP restaurant in Murfreesboro, TN for allowing me to spend countless hours at my booth writing the book and to all the servers who made sure I never ran out of Iced-tea.

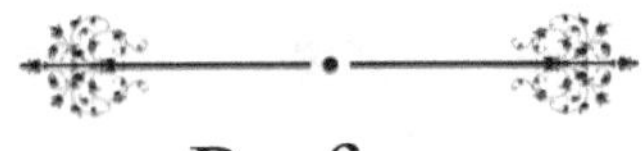

# Preface
The Beginning

It's strange how as when we get older in life, have our own spouses, our own children and our homes we look back and reflect. We wonder and think about how our life compares to the one we had growing up. I look at my children and try to remember what I was doing when I was 7 or 8 years old or even as a teenager. What was my home like? Who were my friends and what did we play? What was my relationship with my brothers and sister? What was my relationship like with my parents? I wonder if there have been any life altering events that may affect them later in life. It's inevitable to prevent life from happening, change will always happen. But the type of changes and when they happen can have very different out comes on a child's life.

Over this past summer my wife and I uprooted our family and moved to another state. My children who are now teenagers have only known one home their whole life, so this change will obviously have an impact on their life. As a parent, we can only hope and pray that we are making the best decision for our family. Unfortunately, we won't know that for some years from now. For me growing up, I too had to be uprooted and adjust to a life altering decision my parents made as well. Their decision was made for different reasons and I believe the effect was far more profound than that for my kids. At least I hope so.

My parents bought our home brand new in 1964. During the 70's more subdivisions and new developments were being built around us. Our neighborhood was quant. It had a grocery store, restaurants, mini markets and even a bowling alley all with-in walking distance. My elementary school was down the street and all the families would use the school's field and playground as a park. It was very common to see people working in the yards, kids playing out front or in the street and neighbors actually speaking to one another.

Our house was located in the middle of the block. My parents would add a second story and since we had the only two-story house on the block our home stood out from all the others. We had a Magnolia tree in the front yard which was awesome because the branches were low and spread apart so it made for the best tree climbing. Plus, the big leaves made it easy to hide and make our fort in it. The rest of the homes were smaller and they all looked the same. Many young families lived on our street so being first time home owners many took pride in ownership. All the homes in the neighborhood were well kept with manicured hedges and nice clean cut grass and no one parked on the street except for visitors.

We knew a lot of the families and the neighbors were all generally nice. However, we did have the typical "Get off My Lawn" grumpy old man that lived a few houses down from us. As kids, we knew to avoid him but it was too tempting to do a door-bell-ditch and run away and hide. He was just too much fun to pester and hear him yell at us to get away from his door.

Our neighborhood even had its own dog. It was an old raggedy yellow lab that only had 3 legs, like seriously. He never went into anyone's home so he really didn't have an owner. As my mom would say, "One day a dog showed up on our front porch and she put food and water outside for him."

He didn't have a dog tag so there was no owner or even a name to call him. I guess because he looked like an old moldy block of cheddar cheese someone thought of the name… "Cheese." It fits.

Every day Cheese would just run around (or rather hop) from house to house and hang out on their front porch or lawn. Pretty soon all the homes in the neighborhood would put snacks out for him. Nobody knew where he would wind up sleeping because he would just wander around our street all day. Every morning would start and one of the neighborhood homes would find Cheese sleeping on their front porch or in the yard. Cheese was the hobo dog and everyone participated in taking care of him.

Well, except for the "Get off my lawn guy." His lawn and bushes were perfect and he didn't like any of the kids near his house. And he especially hated anytime Cheese would wander onto his lawn. He would get his water hose out and spray it at him. Talk about being a jerk. Anyways, he obviously didn't participate with the caregiving. One day, I guess Cheese had had enough of getting sprayed so he decided to leave the man a present in his front yard. My mom said the grumpy old neighbor came outside and yelled at Cheese, "Get the hell out of here" and when he saw the present Cheese left him, he was pissed. He yelled at Cheese that he was going to get him.

Unfortunately, the one time the, "Get off my lawn guy" decided to leave food out on his front porch Cheese being a dog, of course he would eat it. The next day Cheese was found dead in another neighbor's front yard. Everyone knew the old grouch did it. A couple of the dads were pissed and went over to his house and gave the guy a piece of their mind. But since no one really owned him, they couldn't really do much. My mom said that the old man wound up moving a year or so later.

I've looked back at the pictures from back then and my memories were pretty accurate, lots of green manicured front yards with nice bushes and trees. I guess you could say from a visual standpoint it looked like the town of Maybury in the Andy Griffin Show. Unfortunately, we would soon find out, real life is nothing like living in Maybury or like being the Brady Bunch.

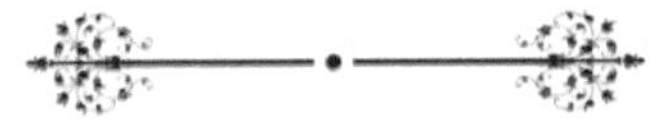

# Chapter 1
## Our Home…Buckner Drive

amilies lived up and down our street. So me, my brothers and sister had friends our ages to hang out with. My older brothers, Lee and Richard were teenagers and they had Danny at one corner and Dan two houses down on our side. Mark lived down at the other end on the corner and Pete lived in the court across the street from us. Next door to me was "Big" Tony, I was "Little Tony." David and Larry lived across the street and Marco (Pete's younger brother) lived next door to them. Beattie lived a few houses down from me on my side of the street and Bennie lived across from him (Mark's younger brother). Even my sister, who was in middle school, had girlfriends on the street. Mark's younger sister Christy (who we called Twiggie), Amy was Dan's younger sister. Deanna was Larry and David's older sister. Lorraine lived at the end of the block and Rosemary just around the corner. So we had our little group and we all lived within walking distance from each other. During this time period kids didn't really stay inside so you could say that our street was busy with kids all the time.

Lee and Richard were my older brothers. Lee was the eldest of all of us and Richard was only a year and half younger than him. They pretty much were inseparable. Lee was the wise, calm and methodical thinker that would love to laugh. Richard on the other hand, if anything crazy was to happen like causing mayhem, getting in trouble with the law or breaking bones, it was him.

Being the youngest with 2 older brothers and an older sister I pretty much had to deal with a lot of crap. I'm sure that's just part of being the younger brother. However, I think my older brothers (and their friends) pretty much went beyond the norm when it came to inflicting pain and trauma. I loved hanging with my brothers and anytime they called me I'd come running. Sometimes it was to throw the football around or help set up the slot car track. Either way, it didn't matter, they wanted me to hang out with them and they were my cool older brothers.

However, just like Charlie Brown would never learn every time he tried to kick the ball from Lucy, I seem to never learn as well. They'd call me and tell me to do this or try that. No matter what it was, more times than not it ended up with me crying and running to mom. All the while they'd just be laughing hysterically so I guess my one job was to provide them with entertainment. My sister was only 4 years older than me so why didn't they do things to her, well, because my mom was a badass (more on that later).

When I'd go running to my mom, I don't think she ever yelled at them, but instead she would give me the big momma hug and kiss me on the head. Then she'd tell me something that I don't think I ever listened to, even in my adult years.

She'd simply say, "Tony, you gotta stop listening to your brothers."

Looking back, had I ever learned to listen to this

advice it would have saved me many years of pain and crying. But hey, as younger brothers, I guess that's just what happens.

# Chapter 2
## Lessons Not Learned…The Dryer

Lee and Richard loved to play with slot cars. They didn't have the dorky small cars, they had the super cool big cars. They would make these huge tracks that literally would cover the entire family room floor. This one day, my brothers and their friends are all playing with the slot cars. I hear, "Tony, you wanna play slot cars?"

Boom, of course I wanted to play. The slot cars were awesome but now I finally get to touch them. Up to this point I could never touch them. If they caught me even looking at the boxes or standing near the track, I was sure to get a smack on the back of the head, a knuckle punch to my arm or a flip to the back of my ears. They trained me well and I learned pretty fast so I made sure to ask before going near them.

But now they actually called me in the family room to play so I was ready. Finally…I thought to myself. After so many years of ear flips, knuckle punches and smacks to my head, I was rewarded with getting to squeeze the trigger and watch my car zoom around the track. Well...not exactly. My brothers and his friends wanted to play Indy 500 so they wanted the sound of cars racing by. You would think they wanted me to make vroom sounds, or hmm like a racing motor. This I would have gladly done. But no, they thought of a more creative way to make the Indy 500 sound.

Typically, when they put their heads together, they usually came up with something that was crazy...like bat shit crazy. They thought the only thing that could make the rumble sound was to turn on the dryer with me in it. Thankfully they at least realized it wouldn't be a good idea to close the door on me. Instead, they just wanted me to put my legs inside and hang out the door. So here I am, hanging out of the dryer door with the dryer spinning and thumping my legs like crazy. I get out after what seemed like forever and with my legs throbbing with pain. They convinced me to do it again and they promised to let me play with the cars. Well, if all I have to do is get my legs beat just to be able to race the cars, then that was a sacrifice I was willing to make. But of course, just like Charlie Brown I didn't learn.

They must have seen my mom coming to the front door because they stopped the dryer and pulled me out. Good, now I can finally get to race the car. My mom came into the kitchen and then the guys decided to leave and go outside. I'm asking if I can play with the cars because they promised that I could play. But they just said, "Maybe later."

Maybe? Maybe? They didn't give me a "maybe" when they told me to get in the dryer. So naturally I did what a kid would do, I went crying to mom telling her they promised, they promised etc.… Well, I'm sure you can figure out what my mom did. She gave me a big momma hug, kissed me on the forehead and said, "Tony you gotta stop listening to your brothers."

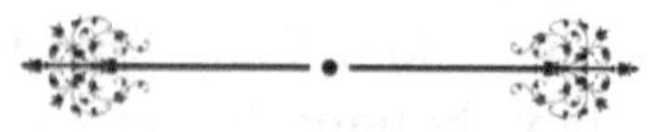

# Chapter 3
## Me and My Friends…Just Played

Growing up in the 80's I guess was a great time to be a kid. Things were far more different than they are today. We didn't just like to play outside, our parents actually encouraged (or even forced) us to go outside and play. We didn't have any electronics and if someone was lucky enough to have a gaming system it was Atari and only had the lame Pong or Tank games. We had way too much fun playing outside.

We rode our bikes and put playing cards on our spokes so we could pretend to be racing on motorcycles. We'd build ramps on the sidewalks with a piece of wood on bricks so we can jump. And of course we'd get yelled at because we always forgot to take down the ramps and the neighbor's cars would drive over them.

We played football at David and Larry's house because they had the corner lot and a bigger front yard. Sometimes we even turned on the sprinklers so we could get muddy and play in the "rain." We wanted to look like the players on Monday Night Football, so before we headed outside, we'd all sneak towels from mom's linen closet. These were great because we could fold them up and put underneath our shirts so it looks like we are wearing shoulder pads. Sometimes we would even put them on our thighs but they would always fall down, so we had to be creative and tape them around our pants.

We played Wiffle ball in the court across the street in front of Marco's house. This was safer so cars wouldn't get in the way. A home run was over the Martinez front hedges. We hated when the ball would go in the hedges because it took forever to find it and whoever did usually wound up with scratches all over his arm. Sometimes we wouldn't find the ball so we got creative and would steal a roll of duct tape from one of our dad's garage to make a tape ball. It was wobbly and didn't fly as far, but hey, it was better than using a rock. We learned that lesson pretty fast.

When looking in the bushes, sometimes we were lucky enough to find a tennis ball. We didn't want to play baseball with the tennis ball because someone, usually Larry, would always hit it over a neighbor's house and we'd always lose it. So we came up with an even better game. It was the ultimate challenge of skill, speed and best of all, it was the most humiliating game we ever played…We called it, "Butts Up." Yes, literally. This game is played in someone's driveway so there couldn't be any cars parked in it. We tried but the owner didn't like us hitting their car with the tennis ball. Most neighbors were really nice so long as we asked beforehand, we could use their empty driveway.

The game is pretty simple. Throw the ball, catch the ball and throw the ball again. But, there are rules to the game. We all stand in the driveway and the person holding the tennis ball would throw it at the wall. The ball has to hit the wall first without bouncing. After the ball hits the wall and bounces back, one of us would catch it and throw it back to the wall…again can't bounce. Also, we need to catch it cleanly and not drop it. Basically, the two main rules are, you can't drop the ball and you have to hit the wall without the ball bouncing. This game was a high stress competition because the rewards were awesome and the punishment was horrible. So as a 7 or 8 year old, this was as intense as it could get.

To play this game, you had to have the basic skill of catching, running and throwing. You had to time your catches just right and catch the ball on a big bounce. Also, you don't want to miss the ball and have to run further back from the wall and risk being too far to make the throw. If a person either drops the ball when trying to catch it or it bounces before hitting the garage door then all chaos breaks out. It's a mad scramble for that person to run to the wall as fast as possible and touch it while yelling "safe." This all needs to happen before another player picks it up, throws it and successfully hits the wall. If that player can touch the wall and yell "safe" they are free from punishment. However, us being kids we'd always make up rules that make it even harder. The person running to the wall can't yell "safe" before they touch the wall because if they did, there was ultimate punishment.

This is where it gets even more chaotic. Say Larry drops the ball or when he throws it, it bounces before hitting the wall. He starts running and then I go to pick it up to try and get him out. If I drop the ball or throw it and it bounces, I have the same requirement so I better get to the wall and yell "safe" also.

So, let's say I do catch it cleanly and successfully throw the ball to the wall before Larry yells, "safe."

Unfortunately, this would actually happen to Larry a lot because he was chubbier than the rest of us and he also lacked the all-important hand eye coordination skills. So anyways, now Larry gets the ultimate punishment and the rest of us get the ultimate reward. Larry goes up to the wall and puts his hands on the wall (or garage door). The rest of us get to line-up at the end of the driveway and get one chance each to throw the tennis ball as hard as we could at his butt. Larry couldn't move because if he tried to dodge or move, we got to throw it again.

At this time, the thrower is safe so we didn't have to worry about hitting the wall or we could even make it bounce beforehand. The game was on pause while we got a chance to put whelps on Larry's big butt. What makes this even more humiliating is, it doesn't matter if he gets hit 1x or if we all hit him, he has to stand there with his hands up and just take it. This game was ruthless. We'd even make up more rules to give us more chances to get someone to have to put their "butts up."

So, remember if a person yelled "safe" before they touch the wall? This was an automatic "butts up" and we'd all get to throw the ball 2x. We wanted to make sure to keep the game legit, no playing around or cheating. If you did this one-time and got caught, you definitely learned not to do it again. We would even make it harder and say you could only catch the ball using one hand. Also, you had to throw the ball with whatever hand you caught it with. So, if you caught it with your non-throwing hand you were kinda screwed if you were too far from the wall.

I remember this one time I caught the ball with my

left hand and I was pretty far from the wall. I knew I couldn't reach the wall so instead of trying to throw the ball I just dropped it and thought my blazing speed would be better. But just in case, I pretended to run into the ball and kicked it off my foot and it landed on the front porch. The other guys called foul and even though I tried to play it off like it was an accident, they ruled 6 to 1 against me so I was forced to the wall for punishment.

We got so skilled that it became fun to try and hit the wall before the guy got to be safe and get the ball to ricochet back and hit him in the face. It was a double humiliation and was totally awesome!!! Some of our older brothers would want to play with us. I think because they just wanted to get a chance to pelt us without getting in trouble by mom or dad. For the most part we'd let them play because we also got the chance to get back at them for always being a jerk to us. But it had to be a group decision...it was our game, so we made the rules. If we did allow them, one rule for sure was that if we did get them out, we all got 2 throws no matter what. The other must-have-rule, they could only catch the ball using one hand. If they were up to the challenge then it was on. They had better aim so we got pelted a few more times, but when we did get that one chance to hit them, we let it fly. Sometimes we hit, sometimes we miss. But either way, at least we had a chance to get some much deserved revenge.

The best time about being a kid during the 80's was at night when we could play Hide and Go Seek. This was the most iconic 80's game of all time. The rule was simple. We could only hide in front yards and in the court between David/Larry's house and Marco's house. We had 5 front yards to choose from so we had plenty of bushes, trees and cars to find the ultimate hiding spot. It was perfect because the street light pole was at the end of the court so that would be base. 1 alligator...2 alligator…3 alligator...all the way up to 20 alligators and then, "Ready or not, here I come." We even allowed girls to play with us, the more people to chase the better. Besides, we're always faster than the girls so it was easy to tag them. However, there is a difference between "tagging" and "pushing" (I'll explain more on that later).

This isn't to paint a picture of glory days, because there's never really been a "perfect" time. No family was perfect and we all had issues going on at home. But being a kid during this time we had a lot of freedom to spend as much time as we could outside. Going from one friend's house to the other and just playing, getting dirty, getting cuts and bruises, but always just playing. Even if some of us would have things going on behind closed doors, when we were outside all together, it was our world and we ruled it.

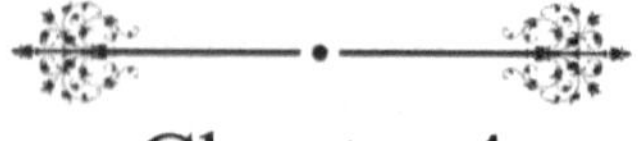

# Chapter 4
## Neighborhood Moms…

Parents were a lot more different during those days then they are now. Actually, I'm a parent and I can say honestly that I am a little different then the way my parents raised me. Typically, all the homes and families participated in the neighbor family. The neighborhood had a "village raises a kid" concept. Most of the parents would let us use the restroom, feed us and even yell at us accordingly. It was simply accepted and actually even encouraged from mom to mom. If one of us would get out of the line, whichever mom was around, would do or say whatever was needed.

My mom was different. Even though kids would have free reign to go from house to house, usually there was always a common meeting point and that house was mine. My mom would always make sure we had snacks and drinks, not to mention we had the only pool in town so naturally we were the "cool" family. Well, my mom wasn't just the neighborhood mom. She wasn't called "Ms. Lombardi" by the other kids,' everyone simply called her by her natural name "Mom."

My mom was an inspiration to me later in life. I didn't realize how much of a pioneer she really was. She was a working mom when she didn't have to be, she ran the house, raised her children as well as all the neighborhood kids and pretty much was the most feared mom on the block.

Our house was always welcoming and I'm not sure when or how my mom had time, but our house was always clean and tidy. We had decorative towels in the bathroom that we could never use. Matching doilies on the couches and coffee/end tables and our carpet always had those cool vacuum lines.

We always had plants around the house and my mom would give them names and talk to them when she'd give them some water. She was kind of quirky and funny like that. Our living room and family room furniture seem to change every month. Of course, the bathrooms and kitchen would get a new color scheme with matching towels, washcloths and rugs. It's funny how as kids we pick up on the littlest things. As I moved out on my own, I found myself doing the same things. I actually liked it.

Now my mom wasn't neurotic like the Mommy Dearest parent. I remember talking to my mom one day about cleaning the house and rearranging. My mom said the goal wasn't to make our house immaculate, it was to make it welcoming and fresh. She liked to do it because it helped her relax and she liked to keep things new because it added to her creativity. I think that was pretty cool. She said the one thing that we can control in this crazy chaotic world was to keep our home sane. There's something refreshing about coming home to a comfortable and clean home to help you relax and decompress from your day.


## SONS AND MOTHERS

Funny story…you've heard the saying that a boy finds his mom in his wife. I met my wife in college and she's been the love of my life for over 25 years. As couples do, when they first start out, they learn about each other and all our nuisances and quirks each other has. To me, this is the best part of having a life partner. I didn't realize this at the time, but my wife is very much like my mom. She takes pride in creating a welcoming home that is warm and relaxing. She has the little trinkets around the house to give our home some personality. I'm not sure how many times a floor needs to be swept or mopped, but our floor seems to never have dirt on it.

I told my mom this story about my wife. One-night when my kids were still toddlers, it was like 2 am in the morning. I'm sound asleep but suddenly I hear this loud *vroom* sound. So, I wake up and walk out to the living room. There I find my wife in the middle of the living room wearing her bra and PJ's vacuuming away. I'm thinking what the heck is she doing? I yell from the hallway and she stops and turns off the vacuum. I ask her the most obvious question, "Honey, what are you doing?"

She said that she got up to get some water and noticed the carpet was dirty. I told her it's 2:00 in the morning and she can vacuum it in the "normal" morning. My mom couldn't stop laughing, because she told me that she was doing that one night and my dad said the same thing. Guess we do tend to be attracted to our mom's personality.


## VALUES

One thing that was unique about my mom was she always welcomed anyone in our home. It didn't matter what race, gender, gay or straight, our home was open and our couch was always a safe place to talk and share. My sister would later tell me that all the neighborhood girls would always talk to mom instead of their own parents if they had a problem. They would confide in her with everything and trust that mom would know what to do, which she normally did.

My mom didn't necessarily share about herself, but she was always willing to lend her ear and offer advice if asked. One thing I know bothered her was when a person was fake or insincere. That would pretty much be the only thing she wouldn't tolerate. Other than that, the person was welcomed with open arms.

I would later learn that one of my mom's good friends was a gay man, which during this time was very taboo. My mom didn't care and she only judged a person by character and not who or what they were. Again, if they were real and not fake, she welcomed you.

I remember this one story my mom told me. We had an open door policy so anyone was welcome and there would be kids running inside and outside of home every day. Especially on hot days, since we had the only pool on our street all the kids in the neighborhood would come over to swim. The family that lived down the street was Black, and the oldest son Lamont was one of Lee's best friends. So, Lamont and his two younger brothers are in the pool swimming with the other neighborhood kids. Our next door neighbor came by and visited with my mom and dad. The neighbor asked my dad why the "Black" boys were swimming in the pool. And as my mom would say it, without hesitation, my dad said, "Don't worry, we put a lot of bleach in the pool."

The neighbor's mouth dropped and then my dad went on to say, "Everyone is welcome in our pool, especially those that don't look like her."

The one thing I have to say about our parents is they really instilled values in us that were far ahead of the norms of families during that time period. Even though I would later learn that our family wasn't the "Brady Bunch," it was stories like this that really made me proud to be raised the way I was.

# Chapter 5
## The Board...Clint Eastwood

Rules from one house to another would vary and whatever the rules were for that house had to be followed by all of the kids. And if we broke the rule, we got the same discipline by that mom as if we were her child. If Larry and David's mom caught us cursing, yes, she would put soap in our mouth. If Beattie's mom caught us running in the house, we'd have to stand with our nose in the corner. And so on, each mom had their own rules and form of punishment. It was tough for us, because there was no consistency so we'd forget what we could and could not get away with from one house to the next. But without question, when it came to my house, my mom didn't play and it didn't matter, we all new to be on our best behavior or she wouldn't hesitate to get "The Board."

Even though there were other moms in the neighborhood, my mom was "THE MOM." She loved all of us, she fed us and of course...she disciplined us. My mom had what was called "The Board." It literally was a board that my older brother made for her because she wanted something to spank us with. He was such a dick. But anyways, this dark brown board hung above the refrigerator. So, every morning when I'd go to the fridge and get the milk for my Trix or Lucky Charms cereal, there was a stark reminder of what could happen when I messed up. Unfortunately for me, it happened a lot.

My mom had a simple rule when it came to "The Board," she'll give us one warning. But when she says those hated words, "that's it," she goes for the board and there is no going back. You're about to get your ass heated up. And it would only get worse if you ran or pulled away. It was bad enough that my mom was the enforcer of all the moms, but what's worse is she didn't get upset. But if we did something really bad like run away or move it really pissed her off, then oh shit did we get a serious red ass and we couldn't sit for hours.

My mom was as bad as you could get. After she said those fearful words, she wouldn't run to get the board. No, she simply would give a nod and stroll to the fridge, reach up and get the board. Even more menacing is when she was smoking a cigarette. She wouldn't put it down. She just kept it in her mouth and let it hang on her lips like a sharp shooter holds a toothpick. I swear when she turned around and started her death walk towards the upcoming victim, you could hear the famous whistle from "The Good, The Bad and The Ugly" when Clint Eastwood would walk into town. You know the sound... "baaa... waaa... waaa... waaaaaaa, drn... drn... drn... drrrrrnnnnn."

She even had the stare like Clint...the cold squint that looked right into your soul. It made you shiver. How could this loving mom who would always give me love pats and kisses on my forehead turn into this? She was maybe 5 feet tall and 100 lbs. She wasn't physically intimidating. It was her walk, her stare and of course the board she held in her right hand that made even the biggest kids turn into toddlers.

My mom didn't discriminate...it didn't matter how old we were, boys or girls or even if we were her kids or not. My mom ruled with an iron fist or rather with a wooden board and not just her house but the entire block. My sister tells this one story in which she and another one of her friends, Deanna, were down at Big Danny's house at the corner with all the other boys. At the time my sister was 11 and she could hang with her brothers, and play outside at the other boy's house, but never allowed to go inside. That was a no-no.

So, word got out that Kerry was down the street and my mom looked out of our kitchen window with the mom glare. If she couldn't see Kerry and the other girls, then she'd walk out to the front yard and if she couldn't see the girls in the yard then it was time for the stroll. I should note that my mom didn't waste time, she was always prepared. So, before she walked out the front door, she would stop by the fridge to get her trusty weapon.

Remember my mom never hesitated, so it didn't really matter how she looked or what she was doing, when it was time to stroll, she strolled. Well on this particular day, my mom was in the typical mom outfit wearing her red robe and had curlers in her hair. Curlers in the hair were a very common mom thing during this time. As if my mom wasn't intimidating enough, to complete her ensemble she was equipped with her cigarette hanging from her mouth.

As my sister would tell it, and later my mom would just laugh when she heard Kerry retell it. Her friend Deanna yelled at Kerry that Clint Eastwood was coming err, I mean mom. Kerry ran outside as quickly as she could, remembering that she wasn't allowed to go inside the boy's house.

Mom starts strolling down the sidewalk and heading to Big Danny's house…the whistling sound begins, "baaa…waaa…waaa…waaa...drn…drn…drn…drnnn nnn." All the kids in the neighborhood just stop moving and look up. They were just hoping that mom wasn't heading their way, even if they didn't do anything wrong.

Here is this little petite woman wearing her red robe, curlers in her hair with a cigarette dangling from her mouth and her weapon in her right hand swaying back and forth. Kerry just stands in the front yard, praying that mom didn't know that she was inside Big Danny's house. Deanna was standing next to Kerry frozen in fear. Mom gets to Big Danny's yard, ever so coolly takes the cigarette out with her left hand and points to Kerry and Deanna and asks, "Were you inside the house?"

As if she didn't already know. By now, we've all learned that we better not lie. We knew mom just asked us to set a trap so she could swat us even worse for lying.

Deanna didn't hesitate. "I didn't, it was Kerry."

Talk about throwing a friend under the bus. But that was mom, she would break the most loyal of friends. She was more feared than being interrogated by the police, at least with the police you'd only have to go to jail. It was worse with mom. My mom put her cigarette back in her mouth, turned my sister around and gave her the red ass. And with each swat reminding the girls "to never go inside the boy's house." After the swats my mom tells her to get her ass home, turns and starts to stroll back to our house.

Deanna just stood there still frozen and probably thanking God that she had the foresight to tattle on Kerry and avoid the red ass. All of the other kids were standing frozen in their yards as well. They just stared at what just happened. They probably didn't want to move because they might catch my mom's eye and draw attention to themselves.

"The Board" became a staple with my mom and the neighborhood. And any time we saw it, we knew it was a reminder of what could happen. She'd even take it to the grocery store. How sad is that...she'd put it right across the top of the shopping cart, so if we were either riding in the cart or walking, we could always be aware that "The Board" was never far from us and always within striking distance.

Some evenings it was a treat when we'd walk down the street to go to the Burger Pit for dinner and then get an ice cream at Dairy Belle across the street. That was a great memory. However, the memory is also tarnished because my mom would hold my hand as we walk and in her other hand, carrying that damn board. That was her 6 shooter she was always holstered and ready to draw. She was the Sheriff, the Duke, Clint, basically she was just mom....and she was scarier than any of them combined.

It may sound like my mom beat us, by no means did she do this. Looking back and reflecting on my childhood, she got in us when we deserved it. Just like I would when my kids needed it. Instead of a board, I had a pingpong paddle that, yes, hung on the fridge. I'm a firm believer that kids need discipline, and when I'd swat my kids, I'd make sure to explain to them why and give them love after. My mom would do the same. Even though my butt was still red and hurt, her little kisses on my forehead seem to always make my pain go away.

Years later I remember asking mom why she hung it above the fridge and not on the wall or in a drawer. She said that since we would always go to the fridge, she wanted all of us kids to see and be reminded that even when she wasn't home, she was always watching...like I said, mom was a badass.

## APPLE DOESN'T FALL FAR

Funny story about one time I was going to get "The Board." I did something stupid, like usual, and I knew it was coming. I thought I had a chance to survive and outwit my mom so I quickly took a bunch of clothes and stuffed them inside my pants to protect my butt. Man, I am smart. This would totally help and I don't know why I didn't think of this sooner. I hear my mom walking up the stairs and I'm excitedly waiting. I know I outsmarted her. But moms being moms, they somehow know everything and are so hard to trick. She opens the door and looks at me. Then to my surprise she told me to take out the clothes or drop my pants and of course I took out the clothes because bare skin with "The Board " would have definitely been worse.

What makes this story funny is with my son. He was 5 or 6 years old and he pretty much did the same things I did as a kid (strange how the apple really doesn't fall far from the tree). Anyways, instead of the "Board" I used a ping pong paddle and of course it too was hung on the refrigerator. My technique was to make my kids wait and think about what was going to come. Depending on what they did, I would work with them and give them the opportunity to negotiate how many swats they'd get. After we agreed on the number then I would give them the choice to either get them all at once or spread the swats out. This day, my son and I agreed on 3 swats and he wanted to spread them out. So, I went ahead and gave him his first one. I let him know I'll be back in 5 minutes and I'd return to do the 2nd one. Finally, I came back to give him the last swat.

For some reason when I gave him his last swat he didn't wince or even cry. His reaction was way different then his first two swats. I patted his butt with my hand and then looked in his pants. All of the sudden I see he stuffed books in his pants to protect his butt. I couldn't help but to laugh inside...I can't believe he actually did the same thing I did. So, reliving the situation as my mom, I gave my son the same option, take them out or drop the pants. Just like me, he chose the better option.

With him standing in front of me, I'm waiting and grinning inside. I can't help but to think how creative this little guy was, so I was kind of proud of him. I rare go back and act like I'm going to give him a big one, but then I just decide to simply tap his butt and tell him that he gets that one for being creative, but he better not do it again. It was so crazy how he responded...he cried worse than the first two times I swatted him. I guess it really threw him off because now he was really confused.

I talked to my mom later that night and she burst out in laughter. She said, "Honey I do remember when you did that."

She then said that she only gave me 1 swat (which was very unusual) because she too thought it was creative. But she didn't have to tell me not to do it again, I just knew not to. Needless to say, I learned another valuable lesson. My mom kept the "Board" visual at all times so we could always see it, but what made us scared is we never knew when she'd reach for it. Fear was the ultimate deterrent…and so is being unpredictable.

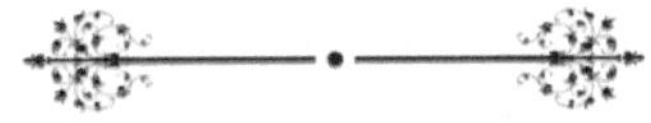

# Chapter 6
Hide and Seek…The Later Story

What was sad about getting the "Board" is if I needed to get whopped, mom didn't mind doing it in front of my friends. In fact, my mom was one of those parents that didn't believe in waiting, she was gonna get in my ass quick. And believe me, she did get into the other kids as well. But judging by how they responded, it was nowhere near as bad as when I got it.

Well, this one summer evening, we were playing hide and go seek. Remember I said there was a difference between being "tagged" and "pushed"? During this game all the kids, boys and girls, were playing. I was the counter so I had to do alligators and then go hunting.

"19 alligator…20 alligator…Ready or not, here I come," I announced.

I already knew who I was gonna chase, had to be a girl. So, I found this girl behind the bushes and of course, she was easy to tag. However, my tag was a little bit harder than expected and she flew into the bushes. Honestly, I may have done it on purpose because as boys we sometimes did stupid stuff like that.

The little girl got up crying and started walking home. My mom was inside but when she heard the crying, she did what all good mothers would do and went outside to see what happened. By now, all of us are standing near the light pole just watching. My mom is bending down talking to her and we see the little stupid girl turn around and point to us (well me) but all of us are standing together. All of the sudden we see my mom stand up and give us a look. The look like somebody just messed up. We saw her walk inside, and remember what I said about when my mom went for the board there was no going back.

Oh man...she walks out the front door and we hear the dreaded whistle, "baaa… waaa…waaa… waaa… drn… drn…drn… drrrrnnnnn." She really is like Clint Eastwood. She doesn't walk, she strolls across the street towards us with her cold as ice stare. Only she's not holding a gun in her hand, it's worse, she's got "The Board." We are all just standing there frozen in fear.

She holds out the board and points to all of us and just says, "Line up."

We are all standing there and I swear I can smell the pee running down my friend's legs. She simply asked 3 words, "Who did it?"

Now, of course I knew who did it. But was I brave enough to admit it? That was a serious discussion I had between my ears. Did I want to risk not being able to sit for like a week because my ass hurt so bad or not being able to play with my friends for like, forever? It was a hard decision, but ultimately, I took one for the boys. I spoke up. But honestly, I'm sure my mom knew before she even went inside to get her trusty weapon.

Without hesitation or even consideration for me telling the truth, she grabbed my arm, spun me around and whooped the shit out me and then told me to get my ass home. I'm running back with tears streaming down my face, snot bubbles out of my nose and holding my burning ass all the way back to my house. I'm not sure if my mom said anything to the others, but I remember when I got back inside, I looked out my living room window and saw my mom walking, I mean strolling back.

I could still see my buddies still frozen in fear standing at the pole. I'm not joking when I say my mom was bad. As kids tend to do, we would make fun of each other, especially when they got in trouble. It's always fun to tease your buddy with his nose in the corner or soap in his mouth. But after that day, the boys didn't say anything, they had empathy for me and just gave me the dude that totally sucked look. They probably were also thankful that I spoke up so they felt obligated to not tease me. Needless to say, from that day forth anytime we were at my house, my friends were always on their best behavior. But to be on the safe side we also decided not to let stupid girls play hide and seek with us anymore.

# Chapter 7
## Lessons Not Learned…Banana Cream Pie

The summer time was generally just chaos because during the day there were no parents at home. There was no-one to monitor us, especially my mom, so this meant my older brothers and their friends would go crazy. Usually, my friends knew to steer clear whenever something was about to get crazy. To describe our house, when you'd walk up to our front door, we had a rod iron fence around our porch. It was actually pretty cool because it was a perfect spot to park our bikes. I would soon find out that the problem with having the fence all the way around the porch is there was only one way in and out.

My brother Lee worked at the local grocery store. One night the grocery store had a bunch of leftover banana cream pies that the employees could take home. Well, this being the way Lee would think...he took home like a whole crate of pies for the neighborhood. During the summer it wasn't unusual to have full on neighborhood water balloon wars, silly string fights or whatever wackiness they would come up with. I'm sure you can already see where this is going…

Anyways, the following day began as normal, whatever this means. What started out as a typical water balloon fight morphed into an all-out war of epic proportions. Water balloons just didn't seem fun enough. So, Lee thought that since they had all of these pies, instead of eating them like normal, he said, "Let's have a pie fight."

Everyone was involved, even my sister and her friends. Our house with Lee, Richard and others was one base and Big Danny's house with the other nimrods was the other base. Lee brought out the whole crate of pies and all the knuckleheads grabbed as many as they could and both teams went back to their homes (or base). I hear Lee count out 1, 2 and 3 and then all hell breaks loose.

By this time, I've learned my lesson, at least I thought, so I just wanted to stay inside and watch through the living room window. I see Lee and Richard's team run out of the house with pies in both hands. They look like a military unit creeping and crouching down between the neighbor's trees and bushes. They were being stealthy as they got closer to Danny's house and then wham, they pied them. They ran back in retreat with Danny's team chasing and throwing pies on the way.

This would happen a few times, Danny's team would ambush Lee's and vice versa. It really was mayhem. Pies were everywhere; smashed all over the street, sidewalks, up in the trees, the bushes and all the neighbor's yards. It looked like that scene from GhostBusters when the Pillsbury Dough Boy explodes all over the city.

As I'm watching this wacky show, I see my brother's team come racing back with Danny's team in quick pursuit. Lee, Richard, my sister and the others get to the porch open the front door and they all run inside locking the door behind them. Danny's team gets to front yard and starts egging Lee's team to get outside and get into the pie fight. When Kerry was racing back, she lost her shoe on the porch.

Danny picks up Kerry's shoe and as if taunting my brother's team, he puts my sister's shoe in the middle of the street and his team walks back to his house. My brothers went upstairs to look out windows and down the street at Danny's house. They ran back down and said the coast was clear. Coast is clear? For what?

I'm just sitting in the living room minding my own business…these guys were nuts I thought. At no time did I participate in this wacky game. I didn't want to play because I knew I would get blasted, and I didn't even like pies, especially banana cream pies. Then my brother Richard, who typically was the biggest tormentor, asked me to go get the shoe. I've learned my lesson now, I said, "No."

My mom always told me, "Tony, you gotta stop listening to your brothers."

So, no way am I going to listen to them this time.

But then Lee, Mark, Christy and the rest of the team are asking me, even begging me. "Tony, no one is as fast as you." "You're Speedy Gonzales." I think I even hear them start to chant my name "Tony…Tony…Tony." Of course, I knew I was the fastest, I had blazing speed. But was I actually going to trust them? Then they said the ultimate, unbreakable word, "We promise we'll let you in."

Well now they promised…this means a lot. It wasn't just my brothers but all of them, the whole team was begging for my help. "Tony…Tony…Tony." So, I agreed.

I'm standing at the front door and surveying my course objective. It was a straight line out from my front door. All I have to do is go through the door, off our porch, sprint through the yard out into the middle of the street and return. Danny's house was way down at the end of the block. No way are they faster than me. I am fast and my speed is unchallenged. Ok, so I get ready. "Tony… Tony… Tony."

My brothers opened the door and I burst out. I'm running so fast that my feet aren't even touching the ground. I bet you could see the jet stream from my back. I'm flying off the porch, through the front yard, jumping the sidewalk and getting to where the shoe is in the middle of the street.

Danny's team must have been hiding behind trees, bushes or the neighbors' cars because all of the sudden I don't hear my name being chanted. Instead, I hear this giant roar, "TONY."

I turn and see these crazed, maniac pie holding kids come barreling down the street at me. It was like I was some prey being hunted down by a pack of lions. I didn't freak out...I knew my speed was unquestioned so I still had time. I reach down, pick up the shoe and start back towards the house.

Even though my speed is blazing I could feel Danny's team closing in on me but I get through my front yard, on to the porch and to my front door in plenty of time. They still hadn't even gotten to my front yard yet. I'm feeling great, I did my job and showed off my awesome speed and quickness. I'm expecting the door to open and my brother's team to welcome me with grand celebrations of my victory.

But instead, no one opens the door. I see my

brother's looking at me through the front door window and they tell me the door is stuck…they can't get it open.

I'm banging on the door and screaming, "Let me in…let me in."

I looked at the living room window and all I saw was everyone's faces just looking at me and laughing. By now, Danny's team had reached our yard and were closing in on the front porch. Remember I told you how our porch was enclosed with railing all the way around and there's only one way out. Now I'm panicking and banging on the door.

"Let me in….Let me in," I screamed at the top of my lungs. "YOU PROMISED! YOU PROMISED!"

There was still a glimmer of hope, maybe I could escape by jumping over the railing and using my blazing speed to get away. So, I run to the corner and try to climb up. My hands grasping the bars and my feet are just about to the top of the rail…but then I feel these hands grab me and bring me back down. And without hesitation or time to prepare myself wham, wham, wham, splat, splat, splat nasty ass banana cream pies are smashed all over me. Everyone on Danny's team just unloaded, it must have been over a dozen pies. I'm stuck in a corner and can't move. I have to just stand there and take it. The whole time I'm just staring at my brother's team laughing hysterically and pointing at me from the safety of inside my house.

After Danny's team celebrates in victory after pummeling a 7 year old trapped on the front porch, my brother's team finally opens the door and joins Danny's team in the front yard. I'm standing there crying and covered from head to toe in nasty ass banana cream pie. I guess the war is finally over, because what was left of the banana cream pies was all over me. Everyone is laughing and full of joy...obviously except me. Here I am the ultimate Charlie Brown and Lucy pulled the football again... urghhhh!!!

My mom will soon be home so the cleanup had to begin because if my mom found the front yard and porch destroyed in a mess, she would have been in everyone's ass. At least that would give me some satisfaction. But for some reason, my brothers always knew when she'd come home, remember the dryer story? So, they grabbed the water hose and started spraying down the windows, the walls, the front door and even the bushes and trees. Of course, I can't go in the house because I'd get mess all over the place so my genius brothers decide the best thing to do was to just spray me down with the water hose as well. I'd just been splattered with nasty ass banana cream pie and now I'm getting soaked. At least they finally let me go in the house to get changed.

I'm not sure how my mom never found out. If she did, I know she would've gotten "The Board" on everyone who was responsible for my torment. But they must have done the best clean up ever because when mom came home it was like nothing ever happened. Just like I said, chaos always happened during the day. My mom came home and I ran crying to her and telling her how my brothers broke their promise and I got pied in the face and drenched with the water hose.

And just as my mom always did, she gave me the big momma hug, kissed me on the forehead and said,

"Tony, you gotta stop listening to your brothers."

You gotta be freaking kidding me mom!!! But for some reason, no matter what happened to me, momma's hugs and kisses always seem to make me feel better.

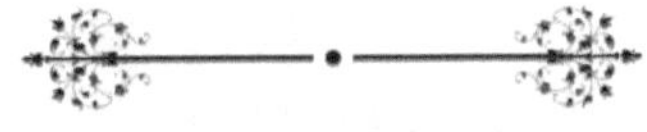

# Chapter 8
## The Dumbasses…The Golf Course

My brother's and their friends would cause a lot of mischief. I'd later find out that usually my brother Lee was the one who would come up with the ideas and of course Richard and the others would follow. Lee was the thinker and he loved to laugh. So, he'd come up with these crazy ideas probably to see if the others would do it and if they did, he'd just laugh his ass off. Probably because what they did was hilarious, but also because he couldn't believe they actually listened to him.

This one summer my cousins had visited us. Anytime my brother's got together with my cousins; Ronald, Raymond and Bill, something was going to happen. And now to have them at our house with my brother's neighborhood buddies also, it was like adding a match to a stick of dynamite. It wouldn't take long for Lee to come up with a crazy ass idea and then the rest of the mindless dumbasses would agree and just go along with it. Usually, this idea involved a lot of pot to be the inspiration for whatever they did.

There was a golf course a few blocks away from our house. Lee came up with this plan to go out late at night, sneak onto the golf course and joy ride with golf carts. Without hesitation, the whole group of cousins, friends all headed out to the course.

They climbed the chain link fence and ran to the garage where the golf carts were stored. Crazy thing is, the golf course left all the keys in the carts so they didn't have to find the keys. They all jumped into their own carts and started racing all over the course. Driving through the sand traps and jumping over the hills and of course playing demolition derby and smashing into each other. As Ronald would later describe it, the goal was to crash so hard to make the other guy's cart flip over. Needless to say, they were pretty successful. When someone's cart would tip over, instead of flipping it upright, they'd just run back to the garage and get another cart. Before you know it all the carts are out of the garage, smashed up and littered throughout the entire golf course.

The next morning, I wake up and I head down stairs. I notice all of my brothers, cousins and their neighborhood friends all sitting at our kitchen table. I also notice my mom just standing there looking at them with the stare that I am all too familiar with. She didn't have "The Board" in hand, probably because of who was standing in the kitchen with her…the Sheriff's department. There were like 3 or 4 Sheriff deputies in the kitchen talking to the dumbasses.

I guess the Sheriff's figured out it was them because by this time my brothers had garnered a reputation that when illegal activity and mischief happened, the best place to start looking would be at our house. But in this particular case it wasn't really hard to figure out the culprit. You'd think with all the stealth planning my brother Lee had, he would have given instructions of being prepared to not get caught. Well, he did. As Ronald and Raymond would later describe it, "Lee told us all to empty out our pockets."

So, they all listened to Lee's wise instructions, except…Richard. For some reason, he decided to bring his wallet and through all the crashing and smashing, his wallet fell out of his pocket. It wasn't exactly like the Sheriff's department needed to do much investigation. The clue was right there on the seat of one of the carts.

They were caught red handed…finally I would see some revenge for the head smacks, ears flipping, knuckle punches and especially the nasty ass banana cream pie incident. My Dad was a volunteer with the Sheriff's department as a deputy and I guess he may have known these guys. Because not only did they not get "The Board " they didn't even go to jail. The boneheads only had to go back to the golf course and clean up, pay for any damage they did to the golf carts and volunteer to wash the golf carts every weekend for a month. How unfair…if I got caught doing something like that, I wouldn't have been able to sit for a year.

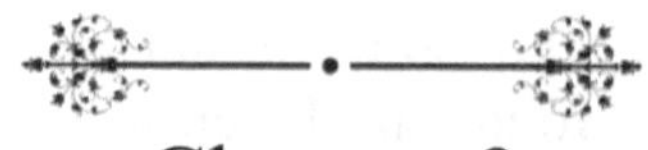

# Chapter 9
## Sporting Family…The Yankee Angels

We were a family that played all sports and usually our parents were our coaches. . All of the neighborhood kids were on the teams as well. Our parents were active with us and all the other neighborhood kids. My dad was the coach of my brother's baseball teams. When it came to me playing soccer, my mom created a cheerleading squad of my sister and her friends to cheer my team on. It was pretty cool, because no other teams in our league had cheerleaders.

My mom, as my sister would describe it, was very tough on all the girls. The one thing she preached was for the girls to be independent and not rely on boys. She wanted them to be strong mentally and know that they can achieve things on their own. My mom thought that sports and competing was a great way for young girls to develop independence and confidence that they could do anything.

East Hills Little League was the league where my brothers and I played baseball. My mom wanted the girls to play on a team but the league didn't allow girls to play on boys' teams and the league didn't have softball teams for the girls. So, at one of the league meetings my mom spoke up and said she wanted to start a girls' team. My mom forced the league to start having softball teams and that season it started with enough girls to make 4 teams.

At the time my sister and her friends were only 8 years old. But that didn't matter to my mom, she made sure they were all on the team even if they didn't want to be. Mom had a saying, "I don't care what you want to do, you're going to do what I tell you to do."

So, with that, the girls didn't have a choice. That was mom. The league grew every year and by the time my sister was 11 there were 10 teams in the league. My mom's vision was a success for all the young girls to believe they can achieve things.

The final season my sister would play would be one of the most memorable times in our family's life. By this time, my brothers were older and didn't play little league anymore so they helped my mom coach. Lee was a real coach, and Richard just wanted to be around the girls. My mom's team, the Yankee Angels, had played 3 seasons together and they were so good that they won the league title every year. My sister played shortstop and dominated as a pitcher and all the girls could smack the ball all over the field. They were solid on defense and overall were a really good team for that level. We didn't have a close game all season and were beating teams like $20 - 2$ or $16 - 3$.

We were East Hills Softball League champs and we were finally able to go to the Tournament of Champions. Teams had to be at least 11 years old to qualify for the tournament and the girls had finally reached that age. TOC's is what it was called and only the teams that won their league could participate in the tournament. It's a tournament in which every State sends a team to play in Texas for the Softball Little

League World Series.

The tournament started out and we started to beat the local teams in our city. Then we started to beat teams in the county. The Yankee Angels team was rolling. They would win game after game from one city to the next. We would travel and play all the league champions throughout Northern California. This was a really cool time because this team was made up of all the neighborhood kids and families so we were all on this great journey together. It was a great time to live in our neighborhood. My mom would later tell the story that she was so proud of the girls because they just kept believing in themselves and wouldn't give up. No matter how close the games would get, they somehow would pull out the win.

As we kept winning the TOC games, the newspaper started to write articles about the team. They had really cool pictures in the sports section of my mom and brothers in the dugout and even pictures of my sister pitching and batting. We were turning into a local sports story. With every game we won, a new article would get printed about our improbable season.

The TOC's were a pretty big deal Nationwide. If you think of the Little World Series you see on television, this was it for girl's youth softball. Each State would have a State Champion and that team would move on to play in Tournament of Champions against other State Champions. We made it all the way to the Northern California State 12U Little League Softball Championship. We were playing a team from Antioch. All the families jumped in cars and caravans on the 3 hour trip.

The East Hills Softball league had only been in

existence for 3 years and here we are, just 2 wins from being State Champions and going to Texas for the United States Tournament. At this point I should say that my brothers were both under 18 and technically they couldn't be in the dugout. Because of this my mom had to have another coach from one of the East Hills teams be in the dugout with her. But he was mainly there to do stats, my mom and Lee pretty much ran the team. When we got all the way to Antioch, they had a rule that only 1 manager and 1 coach could be in the dugout. As my mom would say, "She should have kept Lee." (even though he was under age).

Lee was my mom's calming point, not just in the dugout, but pretty much in everything.

For this game, my brother Lee had to sit in the stands and my mom and the other useless coach were in the dugout. We were a very competitive family and, in this game, our competitive nature just boiled over. Unfortunately for my mom and the girls they didn't have the calming influence of my brother Lee in the dugout with them. We're playing on the road in the city of Antioch, against an Antioch team so naturally they would have Antioch umpires.

All season, my sister dominated pitching. She was undefeated and literally probably had shutouts in almost every game with tons of strikeouts. She threw faster than anyone else and could pinpoint the strike zone. We were ahead 2 – 0 and it was in the 4th inning. My sister had been on fire and struck out several players and maybe only one player had gotten on base. For some reason, when this inning started, the strike zone disappeared. Even pitches right down the middle were called balls. After one walk, ok, maybe things will change. After the 2<sup>nd</sup> walk things started to get real interesting. Now the parents in the stands started to yell at the umpire. We knew my sister was a great pitcher, we've seen it all season long, but now she can't seem to throw a strike? No way, she was getting robbed.

The 3<sup>rd</sup> batter comes up to the plate and my sister throws a pitch right down the middle…and again, the umpire calls it a ball. My sister is now pissed and even though she is just 11 years old she yells and points to the umpire. My mom goes out to the mound to calm her down but usually my brother would do this. My mom walks back to the dugout and she starts yelling at the umpire. I can't remember, but I'm sure it could have been some harsh language. The umpire warned both my sister and mom.

The very next pitch my sister threw was again right down the middle and just as before, the umpire called it a ball. Mom can't go back out to talk to her because if she did Kerry would have to be subbed out. It didn't matter anyway, my sister had already motioned to the catcher to come out to the mound. As Kerry would tell it, "I was so pissed, I told Amy to let the next pitch go and not catch it. If he wants to keep calling balls on me then I'm gonna hit him in the balls."

Kerry takes a big wind up and she throws it as fast as she can. Amy ducks down and the ball hits the umpire right in the goods. He was lucky to be wearing a cup because if he wasn't he wouldn't have been able to walk after that. The umpire jumps up, tears off his mask and emphatically throws Kerry out of the game. He must have known it was on purpose, either that or the sheer embarrassment of being shown up by an 11 year old was too much for his ego. Mom immediately comes out of the dugout and starts to yell at the umpire. The other umpires came to home plate and there was my mom yelling the best 4 letter words right in the umpire's face. Of course, she would get thrown out of the game, but before she walked off the field, she was going to chew their ass out. It was madness. Our parents and fans are beyond pissed as well, but instead of booing mom for getting tossed, they stood up and gave her a standing ovation.

My sister has to leave the dugout and she goes to the bleachers, sits next to Lee who puts his arm around her as she cries in his chest. My mom has to leave the dugout as well but she stands just outside the fence behind the backstop and smokes her cigarette. I'd imagine that had she been equipped with her trusty weapon, things may have gotten really interesting. Mom didn't say a word to the umpire after that, she just smoked her cigarette and glared at him with her stone cold Clint Eastwood eyes. I'm sure he could hear the whistling sound in the background "baa… waaa… waaa… waaa…drn…drn…drn…drrrrrrnnnnnn." He didn't know how lucky he was...he just didn't know.

So now the team is left with the other useless coach and is also without our best pitcher. Everyone in the stands, the players and even mom and Lee knew what the outcome was going to be. It wouldn't have mattered what we did after that, no way were the umpires going to let us win the game. Needless to say, our backup pitcher would walk the next 3 batters and we wound up losing the game...3-2. And just like that, our incredible season ended.

There was a great article in the newspaper highlighting our improbable season. Even though we were robbed, there was optimism because the girls were only 11 and most of them would be able to return next season. We should still have a chance to repeat in the TOC's and this time they'd go all the way.

Unfortunately, that season never came...we never got the chance to know just how good the Yankee Angels could have been.

# Chapter 10
## Road Trips…The Brown Station Wagon

My mom loved to take us kids on road trips. My grandma lived in Southern California and we'd drive down anytime we could get away. One of the most memorable trips we had was when I was 8 years old. That summer mom wanted to take the kids on a trip around the United States. We had the Brady Bunch dark brown station wagon. Because we were a big family and had to bring the dog, we needed as much space as we could get. So, my brothers made a big box on top of the roof so we could put our luggage in it, which is actually pretty smart if you think about it. Crazy how my brothers were such potheads but they still had enough brain cells to think of cool stuff like that.

In preparation for this trip, I thought I would be sneaky and try to hide "The Board." I thought, at least on a vacation trip, we could leave it behind. Mom had this rule that you can't touch the board, but I was willing to risk it. So, during the day when I noticed the coast was clear I snuck into the kitchen, got a chair and reached up to get the board. Success, I now finally had in my hands the very weapon that is used to drive so much fear in others. I can admit, I did feel powerful, kind of like Thor with his magic hammer. I couldn't keep this much power in my hands too long because I couldn't get caught holding it so I quickly found the best hiding place I could think of. I knew mom will never find it and that her weapon will have to stay behind. Finally, I could relax and enjoy myself with a real vacation.

I'm anxious as my brothers are loading up the car and I wait in anticipation for mom to tell us to get in the car. I'm standing in the kitchen just watching mom get her thermos and pour herself some coffee. Is she going to find my hiding spot? I found the best place ever. But dang it, if mom didn't outsmart me again. Moms have crazy super powers beyond my understanding. Either that or I guess it didn't help because when she opened the fridge, she was able to find "The Board" hidden behind the milk. Man!!!! I thought I had her. At least mom took it a little easy on me so my butt was only a little warm.

So now the trip starts out and our first stop was driving down south to pick up Grandma. My mom was one that believed that experiencing education was better than seeing pictures or reading about it in a book. Mom wanted us to stare up at the giant RedWoods, to stand on top of the mammoth Hoover Dam, and to be amazed by the incredible natural beauty of the Grand Canyon.

We went all the way to Washington DC to see the Lincoln Memorial, walk the halls of the Smithsonian and the pathways lined with Cherry Blossom trees. Unfortunately, I was too young to remember much of it, but I've seen the pictures to bring back fond memories. However, I do have 2 distinct memories I can't forget and I don't need to remind myself by looking at pictures. One was the constant smell of my dogs' farts. Ziggy had the smelliest farts and I always had to be in the back with her. And of course, every time she would blow up my brothers wouldn't roll down the back window so I had to sit surrounded by my dog's smelly gas cloud. The other unforgettable memory was the gas station.

I don't know which State we were in, but my sister said it was Oklahoma. We pulled into the gas station to fill up the car. I had to go to the bathroom so when the car was getting gassed up, I hopped out of the car and went to use the restroom. As mom walked inside to pay, I was trailing behind her. I ran to the bathroom and when I came out, I couldn't see mom inside the store. I went outside and now I don't even see the brown station wagon at the gas pump. I look around and then in the distance I see the big box and the backend of our brown station wagon getting ready to turn onto the interstate. Wow, I knew I was the runt of the family but I thought they'd at least want to keep me around.

I remember standing there with tears falling down my cheeks and this old man standing next to me. He had his hand on my shoulder and then picked me up, put me on his knee and we sat on a chair outside his store. I can only imagine what this old man was thinking. But as we sat there, he'd pat me on the back and tell me everything is going to be alright. It's kind of like what a grandpa would do so he became my gas station grandpa. It seemed like it took hours but was more like only 5 minutes.

My sister would tell the story, "I see Tony climb out of the back of the car and run up to the store with mom. Richard finishes filling up the car and mom comes back, starts up the car and drives off. I was a little confused because I knew Tony got out. As mom pulls onto the freeway and starts to head off, as only Lee can do, he speaks calmly and simply asks, 'Mom, did you want to pick up Tony?' Mom immediately turned left on the freeway and drove across the median to go back the other way. She didn't wait for the next exit. She just did a U-turn on the interstate. Looking back, it was funny because poor Tony always got the short end of everything and was always tormented by my brothers and now mom leaves him. No wonder he needed to go to counseling. What's even funnier is when mom pulled back into the gas station, we see Tony sitting on this old man's knee. Mom pulls up and doesn't even get out of the car. She says thank you to the man and tells Tony to get his ass in the car."

At least this time mom didn't get "The Board" out and use it on me. But I'm sure she more than likely blamed my brothers for not telling her before she pulled off. At least one good thing that happened was mom let me come up front and sit next to her. She kissed me on the forehead, I put my head in her lap and she rubbed my ears. Mom always knew how to make me feel better.

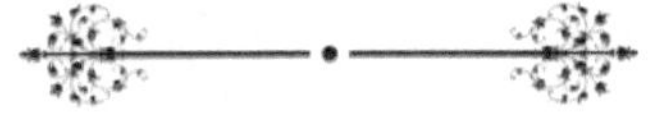

# Chapter 11
## City Kids…Visit the Farm

On the way back from Washington DC we would visit my Aunt and Uncle and cousins who lived on a farm in Iowa. We were city kids. We didn't know anything about a farm except from drinking milk, eating eggs, bacon and meat. When I say farm, I really mean it. I think she had like over 500 acres. They milked cows, raised chickens, pigs and had goats. They were real farmers. This kind of life was totally new to me. This was the first time I've seen any roosters besides FogHorn Leghorn or pigs not named Porky on Saturday morning cartoons.

I remember my aunt had this huge Saint Bernard and I'd ride the dog like a horse. My Aunt and Uncle did things very differently and like most of my childhood, would also make me seek counseling later. For example, this one day my aunt told me to go play with the chickens and catch one. This was cool. Chickens are hard to catch. Even though I had tremendous speed, chickens are blessed with quickness and amazing escape ability.

After a great game of tag and a valiant effort I was finally able to trap a chicken and successfully pick him up and hold him in my arms. I was so proud of myself and I even gave my new pet chicken a name, Charlie. I was holding and petting Charlie and walked over to my aunt to show her my new best friend. She said, "Oh that's a good one," and with that she took Charlie out of my hands by his neck and then chopped his head right off with a butcher knife. Yes, she really did this. Right in front of my eyes she chopped Charlie's head off.

I'm standing there dumbfounded in disbelief and couldn't stop looking down at the ground at Charlie's now lifeless body. My poor Charlie, why did he have to be the one that I had to catch? Needless to say, I was traumatized. My new best friend just had his head chopped off in front of me. I felt horrible, why did I have to be blessed with awesome speed?

Well of course you know what was for dinner that night. Hours earlier I was playing a great game of tag in the chicken coup, holding and petting Charlie in my arms. And now I'm expected to EAT HIM!!! No way!!! On the farm, my uncle had a rule that you must eat everything on your plate. So here I am staring down at my plate of a fried drumstick of what used to be my best friend, Charlie. I can't do it. I refused to eat. This Iowa farm stuff is all way too new to me.

All I remember is my uncle got up from the table and walked behind me and told me to eat. I stood my ground and said, "NO."

Well, that didn't sit well with my uncle, he picked up Charlie's leg and tried to shove him in my mouth. Again, more traumatizing that would lead me to more counseling. I forgot what happened after my uncle shoved Charlie's leg in my mouth, probably because I wanted to keep that memory buried.

A few years ago, when my mom, sister and I were having a great moment of memories this story came up. As Kerry would tell it, "After Uncle shoved the leg in your mouth you pushed his hands away and said, 'Fuck You Bastard.'"

Obviously, I must have heard this from my brothers. Kerry then said, "Everyone is sitting at the table and just stared in silence looking at mom."

Of course, the board still traveled with us, was she about to go get it? It's not like I didn't deserve it. Here I disrespected my uncle, an adult, and in doing so, I even used the best 4 letter word in the dictionary to do it. Not even my brothers would have ever said anything like that, especially not in the presence of mom.

Kerry continued, "Mom never looked up. She just drank her coffee, put her mug down and kept eating."

Uncle stood behind me and didn't know what to do. He looked at mom and asked, "Are you going to allow him to speak to me that way?"

Mom still didn't look up and just kept eating. He then looked at his wife, Aunty Louise, who just shrugged her shoulders and gave a look like what does he want her to do. Uncle pouted and then stomped out of the room.

I guess that day I gotta get out of jail free card. Probably because mom thought he deserved it and was proud of me for sticking up for myself. Either that or because she didn't have to go get the board and whoop his ass for touching one of her kids. As the three of us reminisced at the table while Kerry retells the story, mom just laughs and says she remembers that day. And then mom confirmed my suspicions. She was proud that I defended myself and yes, she did give me the get out of jail free card...just that one time.

Needless to say, I only had mashed potatoes that

night.

# Chapter 12
## The Dumbasses…Together Again

Now that my brothers and cousins; Raymond, Bill, Ronald were back together again it didn't take long for them to come up with some stupid shit to do. As usual, my brother Lee would come up with these ideas and the other dumbasses would go along with it. The good thing for them was since they were on a farm, the cousins secretly grew pot. So now they had an endless supply to get high so the wackiness would never end.

There weren't any stores, malls or even golf courses nearby so there wasn't much to do except entertain themselves. They liked to do experiments and when I say experiments that usually meant what they could do to me to entertain themselves.

## GETTING MILKED

Twice a day, starting first thing in the morning and then in the afternoon my cousins would milk the cows. It was like clockwork and happened every day. There is no such thing as a weekend or day off on the farm. I'd hang around the stalls looking at these big beasts. Not only did they smell, even worse than Ziggy, but they looked enormous and their tongues had to be a foot long.

They didn't milk the old fashion way by squeezing

the teats, they actually had these cool suction cups that they would put on the cow to take the milk out. I'm sure by now you know where this is going. I was scared of the cows. They were just too big so I usually would just hang out and watch the others milk the cows.

As predicted my brothers and cousins called me over to help them and since I always liked to hang out with them of course I was eager to help. Richard asks if I wanted to try it. I'm nervous, but hey my brother wants to show me something. So, he hands me the sucker thing and tells me to just put it on the cow's utter and hold it there no matter what. He emphasized the importance of not letting go because the cow would get angry. I'm holding the sucker and milking the cow. It was actually kind of cool and I felt like a real farm boy.

But of course, this wasn't their plan. My hands are occupied and I can't let go no matter what because I didn't want this huge cow to get angry. My brothers and cousins grab the other suckers and put them all over me. I had suckers on my stomach, head, ears, cheeks and mouth. They seriously tried to milk me and even put the suckers on my nipples. For what seemed like hours but probably only a couple minutes, I was finally able to escape and go crying to mom. And as usual, mom gives me a big momma hug, kisses my forehead and says, "Tony you have to stop listening to your brothers."

I didn't realize this rule still applied away from home. Guess that rule is for anytime my brothers asked me to do something.


## HAY BARN

As you'd imagine on a farm there were barns. They had a really big hay barn and it was cool to go inside and climb and jump on the hay bales. When you don't really have much to do, you create things to pass the time. My brothers thought it would be cool to see if they could tie a rope on the top beam and swing like Indiana Jones from one side of the barn to the other and land in a big pile of hay. They threw down some hay bales and started using the pitchfork and rakes to build a huge stack of hay. Again, sometimes I find it fascinating that for being brain dead potheads they always seem to come up with the coolest of ideas.

They all climb up to the second level, which is like 15 feet up. Richard is the dare devil so if anyone was going to go first it was going to be him. Richard grabs the rope and swings out. He is flying through the air and seriously looks like Indiana Jones. He flies out over the haystack, lets go of the rope and drops into the haystack. He lands and then immediately jumps up and hopping around holding his butt. Someone forgot to put the pitchfork away. Funny thing is, Richard was the one using the pitchfork. So, this bonehead literally flew over the haystack and landed his ass on the very pitchfork he just had in his hands.

Of course, I wasn't allowed to swing so now to hang around them my job was to make sure there was enough hay stacked on the ground to catch them when they'd fall and to never leave the pitchfork in the stack. This one time I'm standing at the bottom with the pitchfork waiting to put the pile back together.

My brothers and cousins yell down to me, "Tony there's a storm coming, look at the clouds."

Living in California, we didn't really get what you'd call "storms" so this was something cool I wanted to see. I dropped the pitchfork and ran outside to see the storm clouds. I look up and don't really see anything. My brothers and cousins were standing above me in the barn loft and they said I could see it better from where they were standing. So, I take a few steps over to my left to stand underneath them and I'm looking as hard as I can.

All of a sudden I started to feel drops on my head but I couldn't see any clouds. I keep looking and then I hear them say, "Look it's raining," but I still couldn't see the clouds.

I look up and I see all them with their wankers peeing on me. Disgusting!!! As Kerry would later say, "I'm looking at Tony through the window and he just doesn't move. It took him a little bit to figure out they were peeing on his head."

Naturally I run away as fast as I can and go get the hose to wash myself off. I go inside and tell mom that they peed on me. Mom gave me a big momma hug, put me on her lap but this time she didn't tell me to "stop listening to my brothers." This was different. The whole time I'm sitting in her lap she just stares out the window towards the barn.

After a few minutes she put me down and went outside to the barn. Mom wasn't taking her usual Clint Eastwood stroll, she was walking pissed off. Ronald said that, "Your mom always scared us when she got that 'look.' She walked out to the barn, looked at us with the 'get your ass down now' stare. We couldn't jump down fast enough and your mom looked at us and simply said, 'Don't you ever do that shit again.'"

Ronald joked that it was a good thing he just peed because if he had any left, it would have run down his pants. Mom didn't just have that effect with all the kids in my neighborhood, her reputation traveled with her.

ELECTRIC SHOCK

To keep the goats in their pins my aunt and uncle had an electric fence to shock them if they got too close. It's electricity, so it doesn't take a rocket scientist to know what would happen if my brothers and cousins would touch it. But they had their idea to see if electricity would run through them. They formed a chain in which they would hold hands and the last person on the chain would touch the ground. This way no one would get shocked. It was kind of neat. It looked cool and fun so I wanted to join in. So did my sister. We joined in and I'm standing in the middle of the chain between Ronald and Bill. Lee touched the fence and nothing happened so it was really cool. We wanted to do it again, so we're all touching hands and Lee touches the fence. This time, for some reason my cousin Bill let go of my hand so I became the last one in the line and got zapped like crazy. I'm dancing and jumping around like my hand was on fire. Naturally they are all laughing.

I don't want to play anymore, but then they said it would be better if I was at the end and touched the ground. They promised I wouldn't get shocked. Ok, I thought. They did promise so they must have meant it. Actually, they did, when Lee touched the fence and all of us touching hands with mine on the ground nothing happened, it was really cool.

Now they came up with an idea that I thought was super cool but soon realized it was ridiculous. They told me if I was touching the car, I could make it start.

So, they tell me to touch the hood of the car and see if it works. I would soon learn though that if electricity touches metal, it will only intensify. I'm sure you can clearly picture what happened next. I'm standing at the end of the line with my hand on the hood and then Lee touches the electric fence. I swear it felt like my whole body got hit with a lightning bolt. I jumped and ran inside as fast as I could to mom. Sitting inside I'm thinking to myself, am I ever going to learn to listen to my mom or am I destined to forever be Charlie Brown?

## TREE TAG

My Aunts property was huge. It had ponds, creeks, open fields and even a forest. One day we wanted to explore and go to the forest. The forest was at the end of my aunt's property line so it was a good distance from the house. We got to the forest and then my brother Richard had to use the bathroom. The house is pretty far away so behind a bush or tree is the best you could do. My brother Richard left the group and decided to drop his pants behind a tree and take a crap. He came back to the group who by this time had climbed up into the trees and were just hanging out. I was too small to really climb high so I just sat on the low branches.

All the sudden, they came up with the great idea to play tag but not on the ground, in the trees. Instead of running around on the ground to escape being tagged you had to stay on the branches. If you were tagged or fell to the ground you "were it." Actually, I thought the game was really cool and looked fun and if I was bigger and a better climber I would have played. My sister was big enough so she was able to play with them. Basically, they were all like monkeys jumping, swinging and grabbing from one tree branch to the other. I could totally imagine this is what monkeys would do and play.

As the game progressed at some point my brother Richard became "it" again. He counts to 20 and then climbs up and starts chasing to tag someone. Actually, Richard was the best climber. He was really fast and probably because he was more risky so he didn't mind climbing higher or trying to jump farther. As the others escape his touch Richard jumps from one tree to another branch. Unfortunately, he tried to out jump his ability because when he reached for the branch, he lost his grip and fell flat on the ground.

Well Richard just didn't land on the ground. Just like with the hay barn incident when he landed on the pitchfork, he just so happened to land in the very same spot when he had to go to the bathroom. Richard gets up and he is covered with his own poop. Of course, all of us are dying laughing. I'm still bitter about the pee head thing so personally I thought it must have been karma.

Naturally the game comes to an end and we make our long trek back to the house. There was no river or water nearby, so as we're walking my brother Lee told Richard to walk further behind us…because he smelled like shit. On our hike back we finally did reach the creek so at least he could clean himself up. Actually, we all decided to swim, but Richard still had to stay down creek away from us. We got back to the house and couldn't wait to tell mom and Aunty Louise what happened.

My mom just laughed and said to Richard, "Honey next time maybe you should go to the bathroom first before you leave."

That's my mom, always with the best and in this case, the most obvious advice.

## FIRE WORKS

That summer we spent the 4th of July with our aunt and Cousins. The 4th of July back home in San Jose was great. All the neighbors would gather together in front yards and the dads would put all the fireworks together. We would even put cones out on the street to block off cars from driving down the street. It was really cool. We had our own fireworks show while sitting in our own front yards. Well at my aunt's house, they lived in the boonies and the only neighbors they had were the Amish people on the next farm. Talk about weird…they always wore black, they drove a horse and buggy instead of a car and forgot about a phone, they didn't even have electricity. Kind of crazy but hey, this whole experience in Iowa was crazy.

Anyways, since there weren't any normal neighbors or even streets for that matter, by the way the roads they drove on literally were dirt. The guys wondered how and where to set off the fireworks. We were at a big farm with open fields, forest and creeks all around us. So, what better way to celebrate Independence Day than to recreate the actual war. Remember they liked to have water balloon fights and who could forget banana cream pie fights. So now instead of hurling water or pies, they thought it would be cool to shoot exploding balls of fire and try to blow each other up.

Like that won't cause any problems. That's right, they bought as many fireworks as possible; Bottle Rockets, Firecrackers, M80's to boom like grenades and Roman Candles to fire like cannons. They had everything they needed to have a full-on war; the environment, the arsenal and above all, the ultra-stupidity to make it all work.

Me and Kerry were allowed to tag along but could only have sparklers, how lame. But in the overall scheme this was probably the best idea. The guys bring out the bags of war materials and they divide them up amongst teams. We went out to the creek which created a natural dividing line (at least that made sense). Kerry and I are standing pretty far away with our lame sparklers but we could still see these knuckleheads about to go to war.

I can't remember who started it, probably Richard, but when the first Bottle Rocket whistled across the water then all hell broke loose. If you could recreate a war battle this was pretty close. You hear the whistling and crackling sounds of the bottle rockets and firecrackers. We see the fireballs from Roman Candles flying across and blowing up on trees and hear the explosions of M80's. The guys were running around from side to side, hiding behind trees and diving behind bushes. It was really cool, especially from our safe spot. I have to say that even though I thought my brothers and cousins were dumbasses, they actually came up with some entertaining things to do, except when it involved tormenting me in some way.

Richard was running from one side to the other and then he dropped his bag of bottle rockets and Roman Candles near the creek. So in the midst of all the madness Richard calls time out. With all the chaos and noise, I'm not sure how they could hear him but everyone else stops. Richard comes out from his cover behind the trees and walks down to the creek to pick up his arsenal. He gets to the creek, bends down and all of the sudden you hear, "FIRE." Richard was on Lee's team, but right now this didn't matter. I actually think it was Lee who yelled it out.

When that happened both teams just started pelting and blasting Richard with everything they had. It was like Custard's Last Stand at the battle of Little BigHorn. Except in this scenario, Richard was all by himself and didn't have support. He had nowhere to go or hide. He was alone and trapped and he even couldn't get his fireworks lit to defend himself. This was awesome!!!

As the full-on assault continued Richard's hair somehow caught on fire. He starts running around and rubbing his head as fast as he could. He wasn't the brightest tool in the shed because he didn't realize that oxygen and friction only makes fires get bigger. You'd think this would have stopped the ambush, but no, it only made it worse. I think everyone else grabbed the Roman Candles, which by the way are basically colored fire balls. You can see these mini colored explosions hitting Richard all over.

Not only is his hair on fire, but now his shirt and pants catch on fire as well. Richard at least realizes he's standing next to a creek so he runs and dives in the water. But now he was like a wounded duck on a pond. All the others came out of hiding. No longer were they firing on each other, they combined forces and just kept blasting Richard while he's helplessly lying in the creek.

They eventually ran out of anything more to fire at him so now the ambush is finally over. Richard climbs out of the water and his hair was smoking and his clothes were covered all over with burn holes. Walking back everyone was laughing at how awesome that was. I have to admit, it was really cool to watch. We get back to the house and walk into the kitchen where mom and Aunty Louise are sitting at the table.

Mom looks at all of us, gives a grin and says, "Well Richard honey, it looks like you got the worst of it."

Everyone else just laughed.

# Chapter 13
## My Brother… "Risky" Richard

As I mentioned earlier, my brother Richard wasn't the smartest tool in the shed. He was the perfect victim for Lee to try for some crazy ass experiment. If there was anyone who wasn't afraid to try anything or even think about the risks beforehand it was Richard. Richard was more of a reactor; he didn't take time to think if it was safe or even made sense. I guess Richard could have used mom's advice of "don't listen to your brothers…meaning Lee." I think by the age of 18 he had already broken his ankle, collarbone, wrist and his legs twice. It didn't matter how crazy the idea was, Richard was up to try it and I have to admit that I do admire my brother's fearless and adventurous attitude.

In no way was my brother Lee a mean-spirited person. He was actually the exact opposite. He just loved to have fun and hang out with his friends, family and find any reason for everyone to have a great time. He would just come up with these crazy ideas to see if anyone would try it. For the most part Lee couldn't believe how these guys even did half the shit that he came up with. But at the very least, they always had fun, even if it came with a couple of bumps, bruises or broken bones.

# TOMATO PLANT LEAVES

Like many teenagers during this time period, my brothers, cousins and their friends were all potheads. Getting pot was a premium and anytime somebody would get their hands on it they would rush to the others and think of creative ways to spark it up. There was no time to waste, getting high was paramount. It was crazy how they thought of all these ways to smoke it. They didn't just use the normal way with a bong or rolling a joint. These guys would come up with all kinds of ways; they would try an apple, potato, banana, toilet paper roll, paper towel roll, 2 liter soda bottle, beer can and pretty much anything they could figure out how to light the weed and smoke it. Again, it's amazing that these guys were actually ingenious with their inventions.

Richard and the others tried to smoke just about anything that had a green leaf. This one time when mom wasn't home, Richard and Cousin Ronald decided to smash up tomato plant leaves. Yes, tomato plant leaves. These were fresh tomato plants so they still had moisture in them. Richard wasn't the smartest tool in the shed, but now that he is with Ronald the two of them combined have the IQ of a moron.

Of course, Lee sees this as a great idea, not to get high, but because these two jackasses were thinking like this. So, Lee tells them that they have to dry out the leaves so they could smoke it. Richard and Ronald both try to flatten the leaves on a plate and they put it in the microwave. As you can figure out, all this did was soften and warm the leaves.

Lee still can't believe what these two are trying to

do so he decides to make it even more interesting and suggests that they put the leaves on aluminum foil to help dry out the leaves. Naturally Richard and Ronald thought it was a great idea. Richard gets the aluminum foil from the drawer and the both of them carefully place the tomato plant leaves on the foil.

I'm sure you could imagine what happened next. After about 3 minutes the microwave starts to spark, catch fire and then boom...smoke fills the whole kitchen. Good thing mom wasn't home. She never was when all this crazy stuff would happen. Naturally Lee is dying laughing as the smoke was so full it started to seep outside. Neighbors saw the smoke and then called the fire department. With sirens coming closer, Richard and Ronald are frantically trying to cover their tracks. They cleaned up the tomato plant leaves, threw out foil and then put a soup can in the microwave.

Mom pulled in just after the firemen arrived and she saw them running in with the hose. The firefighters went into the kitchen and quickly realized it wasn't a fire, it was just a couple of idiots who put metal in the microwave. They said to just open up all the windows and doors to let it air out. Mom walks into the kitchen and sees the two dumbasses standing there and just says, "Clean it up."

Years later when we were all talking about this story, Lee finally fessed up about how the microwave really blew up. Mom looked at Lee and just said, "Do you think I'm an idiot? I knew anytime you were with Richard and Ronald it was only a matter of time before you'd talk them into doing some stupid ass thing to try."

My brothers and neighborhood knuckleheads would try anything that could be considered risk taking. Around the block from our house was this steep road that we all called "Church Hill." My brothers would build these really cool go karts that didn't have engines but they would pull them behind bikes. They'd tie a rope to use it for steering. Again, pretty ingenious stuff. This one day they thought it would be cool to take the go karts up to Church Hill and race them down. The problem was these things didn't have brakes so how would they stop without going into traffic? Actually, they had a solution for that, they would race down and turn into the Church parking lot before the street. Problem solved.

They are doing this and as usual it's really cool. They only have 2 carts so only 2 guys could race at a time. Well Richard spots a shopping cart in the bushes so he decides that he wants to race using the shopping cart. Of course, Lee thinks this is an awesome idea so he holds the shopping cart as Richard climbs in. At the starting line you have 2 go karts and Richard in his shopping cart.

They said go and off they went down the hill. The three of them would start off slow but pick up speed the further along they got. By the time they reached the parking lot, they were going at a pretty good speed.

I'm sure you don't have to be a rocket scientist to figure out that Richard has no way of steering. The other two carts that can steer turn into the parking lot and Richard's shopping cart just keeps going straight. The cart is out of control and Richard is at least smart enough to get out of the cart before it goes into traffic. He jumps out of the shopping cart, lands on the sidewalk and tumbles into the bushes. When he stands up, we all see his hand is turned sideways. He broke his wrist.

## THE POOL

Richard and Lee both loved to build anything they could drive or that had wheels. This one summer day all the guys were swimming in the backyard. Somebody thought it would be cool to build a ramp and jump their bikes into the pool. Our pool was 5 feet deep so if they rode and jumped in from the deck it wasn't too risky. All the guys are riding, jumping and trying to do flips, it was pretty cool stuff. Riding the bike off the ramp into the pool wasn't really that risky.

But, a challenge was then issued. Who wants to jump their bike off the roof? Well of course, Richard was up for any challenge. I should note that the roof that had the best angle to land into the pool was the 2$^{nd}$ story. With the help of a ladder, Richard climbs up onto the second story. Seriously, he's like 20 feet off the ground. All the guys are watching. Richard rides his bike, flies off the roof and then successfully splashes into the pool. From a visual standpoint it was awesome and amazing he didn't kill himself. But unfortunately, Richard kept his feet on the pedals so when the bike landed and went straight to the bottom of the pool all of Richard's weight went to his legs and he broke his right leg.

## THE MINI-BIKE

They loved tinkering with lawn mower engines. They found a mini-bike frame and wanted to build a mini-bike to ride. They would spend the whole weekend building the mini-bike and get the motor running and sounding good.

Richard was excited and of course wanted to be the first one to drive it so he jumped on the mini-bike, pulled the cord and off he went. At first, he is trying to get used to it and driving slowly practicing in the court across the street from our house. But practicing and going slow never seemed to work for Richard. He always wanted to go fast and press things to the limit so he twisted the gas and started to drive out of the court with the motor full throttle. As he gets to the end of the court, he starts to turn but he is going too fast.

He pushes down on the brake paddle and tries to slow down. One problem, they hadn't hooked up the brakes yet. Richard jumped on the mini-bike and rode off before they put the brakes on. He is going too fast to make the turn. The mini-bike speeds across the street towards our neighbor's house, jumps the curb, goes through the lawn and slams into the neighbors' car.

Richard flies over the hood of the car and lands on the other side. Lee and others go running over to see if he is ok. Amazingly Richard is able to get to his feet and stands up holding his shoulder. He broke his collarbone.

## TREE HOUSE

Lee and Richard used to build the coolest things. Like the race car tracks, obstacle courses for their bikes and they even made a fort in the backyard. I'm sure it wasn't for them to play war games, it was probably to sneak girls up or have a private place to smoke dope.

Anyways, we had 3 trees at our house, 2 in the front and 1 in the back and my brothers built cool little tree houses in each one. They'd have ropes, ladders and platforms to sit on. Really cool stuff. The tree in the backyard was the biggest tree and the platform was taller than the first story roof. While they were building the tree house, they were having trouble fitting the platform on the branches.

Richard was the worker and Lee was the architect so he'd stay at the bottom and give directions. Lee gave the idea that if Richard could cut one of the branches the platform would stay. They created a cool pulley system so they could easily bring supplies up. Lee puts the hand saw on the rope and Richard pulls it up. Lee had to go to the garage to get more tools so Richard started to cut the branches.

Lee is in the garage and then all of the sudden he hears tree branches crack and Richard yells so he ran to the backyard and found Richard lying on the ground grabbing his foot in pain. Lee looks up and notices the branch that Richard was cutting...Richard cut the branch that he was sitting on. This is like Benny Hill stuff, you can't make this up. My brother Richard broke his ankle because he cut a tree branch that he was sitting on. Like literally!!!

## ALWAYS BROTHERS

It may sound like I'm being mean about my brother Lee or making fun of my brother Richard, but it's more to illustrate that my brothers, cousins and their friends were all jackasses. My brother Richard had a very adventurous spirit that honestly, I wish I had a little bit of. He didn't mind taking risks because the rewards were satisfying. He had that reputation of pushing the limits and it suited him.

Getting bruises and broken bones didn't scare him. The thrill of the challenge is what he lived for. It's not that I didn't love my brother. Even though he was my main tormentor growing up, he still looked out for me. He would encourage me to press my limits and later on I would, but not to the extent of him. As we both got older at some point, I was no longer his pest little brother, I just became his younger brother.

# Chapter 14
### Returning Home…The Door

The trip took us the entire summer and my Aunt and Uncle's farm was the last stop before we started our trip home. Aside from the Iowa farm visit, I don't recall much of the other places but I have seen the pictures. Actually, as a parent myself, I think it would be a really good family experience for me and my wife to do with our kids. We finally made it back and I was still too young to recall exactly what happened but my sister was able to fill in the story.

As my sister would tell it, "We pulled into the driveway and got out of the car. Lee, Richard and Cousin Raymond were unloading the car. I walked with mom to the front door and the strange thing is, the front door was locked and we never locked the front door during the daytime. Mom unlocked the door and walked in. Right away I noticed a purse sitting on the yellow chair in our living room and wine glasses on the coffee table. I distinctly remember the pungent smell of perfume and it didn't smell anything like mom puts on. Mom turned to us kids and said to wait outside. Mom walks up the stairs and she doesn't notice I'm trailing behind her. She opens their bedroom door and I see the neighbor lady from down the street under the sheets in mom and dad's bed. Then I see dad come out of the bathroom wearing his robe, he turned pale white and just froze. Mom stared at dad for a moment. Then she simply closed the door, took me by the hand and said, 'Let's go.'

"I didn't know what happened; I just remember having this weird feeling inside my stomach. I just held mom's hand tight and walked down the stairs with her. We walked through the living room and out the front door. Lee, Richard and Raymond were all standing on the front porch with our luggage and mom told them to load it back up. As the boys put the suitcases back into the box on top of the station wagon, mom just sat in the car. I sat in the front seat next to her because mom was still holding my hand. Looking back, I'm sure I was the only thing that she could get support from at that moment. The boys finished loading the car and we drove to Grandma's house. For the entire 5 hour drive, none of us kids said a word. That was the longest and loudest drive in silence I've ever had."

To this day I hate to hear Kerry tell this story. It's strange because it took many years in adulthood for any of us to talk about it. And some of us would still even avoid the subject. Our world changed at that moment. All our lives would forever be altered. The life path we were on as a family and as individuals abruptly changed. This event affected all of us differently. I was still very young, my sister was getting close to being a teenager and up to that point, both my brother's had lived their whole life on our street. They had friends all over the place and everything they knew and cared about was within walking distance. I can only imagine how bone crushing this was on them. My brother Lee was different, he was similar to my mom with how to deal with things as they come. However, for my brother Richard, it seemed to haunt him. Even though he had a career, bought a house, got married and had a child, he seemed to really never leave Buckner Drive.

## THE LAST GOODBYE

A week or so went by and we came back from Grandma's house and mom decided to stay for that school year. This is where me and my sister lived in a complete fog because neither one of us recall ever coming back from Grandma's house. After that school year, mom decided that it was time to move on and like so many families during this time, our family fell victim to our parents getting divorced.

Not only did this change our family but the entire neighborhood. I remember when we were loading up the car and getting ready to leave it seemed like every household was standing around our driveway with people overflowing into the street. There were people from the baseball league, friends from school and mom's work. Hugs, kisses and tears were on everyone's face. I remember some years ago running into a neighbor that grew up with us and we got to talking. We chatted a bit and somewhere in that conversation I could see his eyes focus as if he was looking back in time. He got teary eyed and said, "Man things sure did change after we left."

It sure did...for our family, for his family and for all of the families that lived on Buckner Drive.

Communication was limited growing up. We pretty much just did what we were told to do. If it's one thing about my mom, she didn't really share too much. She was a tough and strong-willed person and she'd simply say things like "that's life" or "you have to just keep pushing forward." I'm sure my mom was hurting, the same as us kids but we just didn't talk about it until many years later. And even then, the wounds were still fresh like it just happened that day. It's very sad to think of how precarious and fragile life can be and simply opening a door can literally turn your whole life upside down.

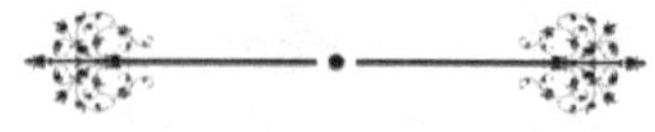

# Chapter 15
## The Move...Niangua

A few months after we returned from our summer vacation, my aunt, uncle and cousins moved from Iowa to another town in the middle of nowhere. They moved to Elkland Missouri and even talked Grandma into moving with them. Mom thought that it would be good for all of us to be surrounded by family so we decided to move to Missouri.

Mom bought us a home in Niangua, Missouri. If you've never heard of this place, it wouldn't be a surprise it's literally like a speck on the map. We probably had more people that lived on our block in San Jose than the total population of Niangua. Last summer we visited my aunt and uncle in the middle of nowhere, and now we are going to "live" in the middle of nowhere?

Being around the cousins helped with the culture shock, especially for my brothers and sister but for me, it was still a little different. One thing for sure is I knew not to get attached to any of the animals they had on their farm. The last thing I needed during this time in my life was to have another Charlie incident.

Our home was about 30 minutes from our aunt and uncle's home. I'm not sure why we couldn't find a place a little bit closer but I guess mom wanted to be even more isolated. Driving to our home was interesting because the roads didn't have names, they only had numbers, like Highway 97 or Road HH. Not sure why they couldn't decide on real names but I guess because they probably only had like 5 roads in the whole town so it was probably easy to remember. It got even more interesting when the road turned into dirt.

We pull off the road and turn into this rock driveway and mom says this is it. This is our new home. But for some reason we can't even see it. The only thing we could see was the roof and a chimney. From the rock driveway to the chimney all we can see are bushes and weeds that were taller than me. Even though I'm still pretty short, imagine weeds tall enough that you could get lost and not be able to find your way back. That was our "new" house.

At least mom was prepared because she brought tools and cleaning supplies. We had to chop a path in the weeds to finally get to our front door. As my sister would say, "It was the craziest thing. We're all standing in a line behind Lee and he is using a machete to chop down the weeds and make a path for us."

Finally, we get to the front door of our home and all I remember was it was dark and empty. It must have been sitting empty for years because it had cobwebs everywhere so we had to do a serious cleaning before we could even start bringing in our stuff.

We spent that summer getting our new home ready. We painted inside and out. Lee and Richard built a patio and mom put in new carpet. Mom made the best of our situation and still was able to make our house comfortable and as warm as it could be. Of course, she had her plants, doilies and towels so even though our outside address changed, the inside still felt the same. Like mom's philosophy we just keep moving forward and make the best of our situation.

Our property would be considered a small farm. It was a little more than 40 acres, had 4 old barns, a couple of ponds, open fields and similar to the farm house in Iowa, we had a forest at the far end of the property. For a city boy coming from sidewalks and manicured front yards this was definitely a culture shock.

## NEW FAMILY

At least mom did have the foresight to move us closer to relatives so the one good thing about moving to Niangua was we did live closer to our cousins, Aunty Louise and Grandma. Not so much my uncle, but I think he learned his lesson so even when we visited each other, he and I weren't really in the same room together.

I especially loved my grandma. When we lived in California, I would see her for holidays and maybe a few times a year. But now that she lived closer to me, I actually got to visit her all the time. During this time mom really leaned on Grandma. Just as mom always knew how to make me feel better, I think Grandma knew how to make my mom feel better. I would later come to learn that it doesn't matter how old or mature we become, we will always be our momma's child and she will always be our mom. Things just never change, and honestly, it's the way it should be.

Just as back on Buckner, our home soon became the hub. I remember our house always seemed to be filled with people. This was interesting because it wasn't like people could just walk over, they pretty much had to plan and drive over. Friends and family would be over often and the laughter and company is what we all needed during this time.

One thing that was great was for the first time our families could spend all the holidays together. Not to mention celebrate all our birthdays together. So, since I was the youngest of the family, I would get double and even triple the gifts so I seem to make out every year. From this standpoint, those are very fond memories for me.

## THE NOT REALLY NEIGHBORHOOD

Moving to a small town as a 9 year old was tough. Last summer we went on an awesome road trip that included visiting my aunt and uncle's crazy farm in Iowa. I thought I left that crazy place forever and now I'm expected to transition from city boy to now being a farm kid? Talk about a new adjustment. I went from having my friends living next door, across the street and down the block to now not having anybody living close by. To give you an example, the only kid my age lived like a mile away on a corn farm and what's worse...she was a girl.

My sister made friends pretty easily. She was lucky because a girl her age lived down the road from us. Her name was Rhonda and she wasn't just my sisters' best friend she would soon become part of our family. She was really nice to me, but her family was crazy. I thought the Amish people that lived next door to my aunt and uncle in Iowa were strange. Rhonda had a big family with 5 older brothers and a younger sister. So combined with her mom and dad, there were a total of 9 people living in the house. The weird thing is, they lived in a 1 bedroom house and you could almost categorize the house as more of a shack. I've never seen anything like it before. It looked like something my brothers would make in our backyard.

The neighbor in the other direction lived in a mobile home and we didn't really know him. We just referred to it as the house with all kinds of stuff in the yard. It looked like they collected junk or something. Actually, thinking about it, almost all the homes around us seem to collect their own junk piles in some sort of way. I would soon understand why the neighbors would accumulate stuff.

Living out in the middle of nowhere was an adjustment for all of us. When we lived on Buckner Drive, I guess you can say we had an easy life. Everything we wanted was all around us. Now everything was different. Even though we visited my aunt's farm last summer, we didn't "live" on the farm. In Niangua, we uprooted all the conveniences of city life to now having to learn how to do things on our own. We had to make adjustments to everyday things. No longer could we just walk to the restaurant down the street, we didn't even have a street. Couldn't play hide and seek because we didn't have light poles to act as a base. The grocery store wasn't a simple drive, it was 45 minutes away and we had to plan ahead and buy enough to last us a month.

I don't want to make it sound all bad, it was just different. The older I got the more I learned to appreciate and understand my mom's words of wisdom. "That's life, you have to keep moving forward" or "when tough times look you in the face, you stare right back at it."

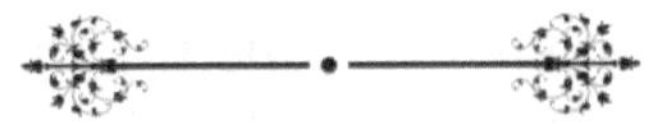

# Chapter 16
## County Living...Animal Farm

For some reason, since we lived on a farm mom thought we might as well become farmers. I guess mom figured we loved our experience in Iowa that we could do it. After a few months of living at the new house Mom bought us a cow, a couple of pigs and a few chickens. Obviously, I was leery about the chickens, but mom did say we weren't going to eat them, we just wanted the eggs. This was kind of smart because the grocery store was pretty far away.

Every day my job was to go out to the chicken coup, feed and water and search the nests for the eggs. It was like going on an Easter Egg hunt every morning. Sometimes mom let me open up the coup and let the chickens roam around. It was actually cool to see chickens just walking around your backyard. They never really wandered off too far and when it was time to bring them back in, you just shake up the bag of seed and throw it on the floor of the coup. I felt like a real farm boy.

Mom bought the cow for milk, but we didn't have the sucker machine and it was way too hard to milk the cow the old fashion way. So now we have this 2000 pound cow that just eats and poops all day long and we don't get anything useful for all our hard work. Except for mom, now she had a pet and the cow would now be called Momma Cow. I could relate to mom, because just like me and Charlie, she and Momma Cow became best friends. But unlike my Charlie, Momma Cow was going to be safe and didn't need to worry about getting chopped up and eaten for steak.

Everyday mom would wander out to the barn and check in on Momma Cow. Mom would give her feed and water but mostly mom liked to just pet and talk to Momma Cow. As kids, our job was to clean the stall, feed and water and make sure she had enough hay to lay-down in. Basically, we still had to do all the grunt work. This one time when Kerry went out to feed Momma Cow, Kerry found mom sleeping side by side in the hay with Momma Cow. I guess mom really did find her new best friend.


## THE PIGS


The pigs were another story. Mom came home one day and she had 2 little piglets with her. Since my job was the chickens, Kerry took care of the pigs and we both shared the responsibility for Momma Cow. The piglets were so cute and Kerry and I would run around and play with them all the time. But these piglets ate so much that they became enormous pigs. No longer could we run around and pick them up, every time we would go into their pin, instead of us chasing them, they started to chase us. We would soon figure out why.

Even though they looked cute and cuddly when mom first brought them home, we would soon find out that they must have been spawned by Satin himself. As Kerry would give them the name "Evil Pigs."

When Kerry would take her first steps inside their pin, they instinctively knew she entered their domain. They would turn around and sprint to her as fast as they could. These beasts were not small, they had to weigh over 800 pounds each with huge heads and mammoth snouts. They would chase Kerry and if they caught her, they would chomp down and pull on her shirt. It was as if they were playing football with her and tried to tackle her to the ground.

This would happen every day and I felt bad for Kerry, but I'm too small to help her. Even though I was blazing fast, if I tripped or fell, these beasts would have eaten me for a snack. One day, Kerry asked if I could help her. Of course, I would do anything for my sister. She asked me to go on the other side of the pin and try to distract the pigs. This was a great idea. I could at least use my speed, but would be safe because I'm on the outside of the fence. I kept yelling at the pigs to draw attention to myself and Kerry was able to get in and get out without stressing of being eaten by the Evil Pigs from Hell.

So, from now on, when it became feeding time for the Satin's Pigs, Kerry and I would work together to do the job. But just like earlier, these beasts are smart and pretty soon they caught on to our gig. This one day I'm distracting the pigs and they are looking at me, grunting and snarling like usual. Kerry steps out under the fence and as soon as she gets all the way to their feeding trough they turn around and start running right at Kerry.

It's like they planned and knew exactly what they were going to do that day and they wanted to wait until she was far enough inside the pin before ambushing her. Kerry freaks out, throws the feed in the air and turns around sprinting to get out of the pin as fast as she could. From that day on, Kerry didn't want to chance it again so she would just throw the feed over the fence.

Ultimately the Evil Pigs would get so big that mom would have to get rid of them. When mom's friend came in his truck and loaded the huge, monstrous, fat bellied pigs, Kerry and I didn't cry one bit. Actually, I think Kerry even offered to help load them up. Funny thing would happen a few days later. That same friend would return with a lot of packages wrapped in white paper. Mom got the packages and placed a couple in the refrigerator and the rest in the freezer.

Later that night we had pork chops and mashed potatoes for dinner. It didn't take a rocket scientist to figure out what happened to the Evil Pigs from Hell. But you know what, instead of being traumatized like the Charlie story, I have to say those were the best pork chops we've ever had. I also looked over at Kerry, and I think she enjoyed every bite because she couldn't stop smiling as she chewed. I think she even had seconds and thirds She must have been really hungry…either that or she was enjoying the ultimate payback.


## HADDIE


We didn't just have farm animals on our property. My brother Lee also had this black mangy dog named Haddie. Haddie was fun to play with and when I didn't have my imaginary friends, she would always play with me. Which was fun, because if I threw the ball, she would at least bring it back.

From time to time, Haddie would leave our property, which isn't really surprising because we were surrounded by fields. However, she was a scrounger and when she returned, she usually would be carrying something. She would come back with pretty much anything she could carry in her mouth and place it on our front porch. The problem is she would always get the stuff from the neighbor's house down the street. Clothes, pots, pans, tools and one day she even brought back golf clubs.

It became a running joke because whenever Haddie went missing, we knew where to find her. We'd just wait until she returned carrying something and we'd walk it back down to the neighbor to return it. The neighbor was a nice older man and he didn't mind, he actually found it amusing.

Along with scrounging the neighbor's house, the next best thing for Haddie was chasing anything that moved. And being on a farm, there were a lot of animals for her to chase. She'd see squirrels, gophers, jackrabbits and go chasing. Anytime we let the chickens out she loved to run around and chase them also. The only animals she knew not to mess with were the Evil Pigs. She wisely stayed away from them.

One time, we couldn't find Haddie so we were waiting to see what treasure she would bring us that day. We started to smell something from the front yard but living on the farm you would always have strange smells. However, this was a very distinctive smell…it was the pungent smell of a skunk.

Lee goes to the front door, opens it up and looks down. There is Haddie with her latest gift in her mouth.

Yep...she successfully caught a skunk. It was so nasty. The smell wreaked and not only that, Haddie wreaked. Lee had to carry the skunk and throw it across the road. And he had to spray down Haddie with the soap, tomato sauce and water like 10 times before getting some of the smell away. It was an experience, but sadly, not the most unfortunate surprise we would later get from Haddie.

Kerry had a friend named Marple. He was a big, lovable guy and he and Kerry were very good friends. One day Marple visited our house and was talking to the family for a little bit and then he told Kerry he had a surprise for us. In the country it is very common for people to go hunting. Marple loved to go hunting and on this day, he wanted to show us what he shot earlier in the morning. We go to the front door, walk outside and then Marple starts to look around on the front porch.

All of a sudden we see Haddie running around the front yard with Marple's dead rabbit in her mouth. We all felt horrible for him. He was so proud that he spent all morning hunting and now he sees his trophy flipping and flopping in Haddie's mouth. Marple was crushed. Mom tried to be nice and rubbed his back telling him she appreciated the gesture. Dejected, all he could do was just say he had to go and he walked to his truck and drove off. Marple and Kerry remained close all through high school and he still visited the family. But needless to say, anytime Marple went hunting, he decided not to share his trophies with us anymore...I don't blame him.

# Chapter 17
## Life In the Boonies…Trash Story

There are no garbage trucks so we had to dump our own trash in a big round metal bin in our back yard that we would aptly call "The Burn Barrel." Once the barrel got filled, we would have to burn our own trash, seriously. Good thing this wasn't during this time period with all the climate crisis wackiness. Activists would have gone crazy about burning trash.

Burning trash was a new experience for all of us. Back on Buckner, all we did was take our trash cans to the curb and let the garbage trucks dump it for us. How the heck do you burn trash? Well, we knew how to build a fire, but to build a fire to burn garbage? Mom thought for the first time that Lee would be better to show us how to do it. Ideally Richard would have been the one to try it, but mom probably thought he would blow himself up or something like that. The burn barrel was pretty big, like the size of our pool on Buckner so it would hold a lot of garbage, probably a few months' worth.

It's getting close to winter because the ground is frozen. We are all standing inside the kitchen looking through the window and Lee walks out with his army jacket over his robe while wearing his combat boots. This was a cool first time experience for all of us. So, we're all watching and trying to figure out what he is going to do. So, Lee takes this can of gas and starts to sprinkle the gas around the burn barrel. Seems smart, he needs something to help ignite the flames. Well apparently, Lee had sprinkled a little bit too much.

You think Richard would have done what comes next. Instead of lighting a piece of paper and throwing it in the barrel, Lee reaches down inside the barrel using his lighter to light it. All of a sudden we hear this explosion and it looked like a bomb blew up with huge flames in the sky. The house shook and the blast was so big that we could even feel the rush of heat through the windows. Smoke filled the whole yard and then we saw Lee running as fast as he could back to the house.

Lee made it back inside and I guess in some sort of irony from the Richard firework story, he was on fire. Not like flaming, but his hair was smoking, his eyebrows were missing and his long beard was sparkling with little burn marks. At the time, Lee had a really long ZZ Top like beard but after that day he probably lost 3 or 4 inches from its length. He runs to the kitchen sink, turns on the faucet and puts his whole head underneath the water. After a few minutes of washing his hair and face he turns around dripping wet and then mom hands him a towel.

Now that we see it is ok, we all start busting out in laughter. Even mom thought it was humorous and just as mom could only say, "Well Lee, honey it looks like we now know what not to do."

We keep laughing...

# Chapter 18
### Seasons Change…Adapting

Not only were we adjusting to a new home, new location, new surroundings and new people, one of the biggest things we had to adjust to was new weather. Back on Buckner the weather was pretty mild. There were more sunny cloudless days, minimal rain and definitely not very many cold days. The great thing about the weather in San Jose is our outdoor play time activities were not really impacted by the weather so what we played in June, we also played in January. The only real activity we couldn't do was swim in our pool, but what's crazy is there were even days in December where it was still warm enough to jump in the pool. The weather didn't fluctuate too much from one season to the next. Actually, in San Jose, there pretty much was only 2 seasons, summer and a mild winter. For us to experience snow we would have to drive 4 hours up north to Lake Tahoe.

Well in Niangua Missouri, 4 seasons happen every year. You could pretty much set your calendar on the months when you would start to see the seasons change. Rain would start to come in March along with the allergies from the springtime blossoms. Summer would start in June and become unbearably hot, sticky and muggy. Leaves would start to turn colors in September. And finally in December the temperature would get cold enough that we would get some snow days. Coming from San Jose, I have to say that it took a real adjustment, but at the same time, it was kind of cool to see how the climate and environment changes every 3 months. But never before did I have to wear snow boots, gloves, beany hat and a big puffy jacket on my way to school. I seriously looked like that kid on the Christmas Story movie.

## SUMMER FUN

Our first summer was also the first time we would feel heat and humidity but unfortunately, we didn't have a pool to jump into in our backyard. By this time, we have become a little acclimated to the country life. We had to come up with creative ways to use whatever we had around us. We had 2 ponds on our property so we kind of had our own natural pools. However, if you've never heard of snapping turtles, they are very real. These are turtles that love to live in mossy waters because it's easy for them to catch bugs and whatever else is stuck on top of the water.

Obviously coming from the city, we've never seen or heard of a snapping turtle. It didn't take long for us to figure this out. One hot day we decided to walk to the pond near our house. I should note that it was just us kids, no cousins or neighbors to give us advice. So, we get to the pond and of course Richard being Richard just jumps in. Me and Kerry are just walking around the edge of the pond getting our feet wet. Soon after we see Richard jump and say something bit him. But instead of him coming out of the water he decides to investigate further. He starts looking in the water and then he jumps up, yelling and running out of the pond. Richard wasn't wearing a shirt and when he was looking down in the water a snapping turtle came up and bit him. He jumps up and starts running out of the water with a turtle hanging off his chest and another dangling on his cutoff shorts. He gets to the shore and literally has to use both hands to pry the mouth open to get it off his chest. When he finally does, he has a bite mark and bleeding just below his nipples. I'm laughing and Kerry is laughing so hard that she actually peed her pants. It was that hilarious.

We finally learned how to adapt to our environment so now we wanted to find things to do. We knew we couldn't swim in the pond, but we found this really cool river down the road from us to swim in. It was a little bit of a walk so we would have to plan ahead. Similar to the hay barn, my brothers tied a long rope from one of the trees so we could fly out and drop in the water. Sometimes on hot days we would see kids from all around and there would be like 15 or 20 kids swimming and swinging from the rope. This was a great memory.

## WINTER FUN

The winter time gave the guys an opportunity to be more creative with different ways of using, or tormenting me. But at least this time, my sister was involved with me. During the winter time it would drop below freezing and our ponds would freeze over. None of us have experienced this so naturally it was pretty cool. One day when it was frozen, we checked to make sure the pond was solid enough for us to walk on and then we started to run around and slide on it.

But running around and sliding wasn't fun enough

for my brothers and cousins so they thought about racing. Not by running across the pond, but by sledding across. But we didn't have any sleds so my brothers went to the house and got a couple cardboard boxes. How are they going to use these as sleds? Well, they had a simple solution for this they also brought back some rope with them.

They looked at me and Kerry and asked if we wanted to play. Of course we did, my sister was usually just as excited as me anytime my brothers or cousins would ask us to do anything with them. So, they took the rope and tied it around our waist. They said we had to pull them around first and then they will pull us after.

So, me and Kerry are standing there on a frozen pond with a rope tied around our waste and Richard and Ronald sitting in their sled boxes behind us. Lee yells out, 1...2...3 GO!!! Me and Kerry start to move our legs and try to run as fast as we can but all we are doing is sliding and falling and can't pull the box. My brothers and cousins must have failed physics because when you have a 50lb person standing on ice with no traction trying to pull a 150lb person it doesn't seem to work.

No problem, they had a solution to this as well. Richard and Ronald run inside the garage and come running back to the pond. I guess they really were excited about trying to race. Either that or they wanted to see if they could solve the problem with their goofy idea. When they get back to the pond, they are now holding a hammer and some nails. Yep…you figured it out. They took off our shoes and hammered nails into the bottom of them.

Neither one of us complained because we were still getting the chance to play with them. So, we get back into our starting positions with ropes around our waste and Richard and Ronald sitting behind us in their self-made sled boxes. But now we have traction on our shoes. 1…2…3…GO!!! At first, it was really difficult but once we got one step in front of the other, we were actually pulling the guys. We eventually got running and since I had more blazing speed me and Ronald were winning.

We spent hours pulling everyone around on the pond and when it was finally time for me and Kerry's turn, they said they were tired and went inside. Tired? How could they be tired, all they were doing was sitting on their ass while Kerry and I were playing sled dogs. So now we both are dejected, we spent the whole morning pulling these guys and we were fooled again. But at least this time, Charlie Brown wasn't alone.

# Chapter 19
## First Winter…Kitchen Table

Adjusting to our first winter was a whole different story. We didn't have an electric heater or wall furnace. To heat our house, we had to make a fire in the chimney. Our chimney back in San Jose was just for looks, we never built a fire. Again, this whole Missouri experience was new to us and we didn't really know what to use or even to make a fire. But at least we did learn from the Lee burn barrel incident of what not to use to light it.

As I mentioned, seasons in Missouri are like clockwork, however in our first winter our clock was broken. People think farmers are not very smart, but I can tell from firsthand knowledge that farmers have far more common sense than city folk. Trees are everywhere in Missouri so trees created a natural warming element. So, beginning in the fall months, people cut down trees to prepare for the winter. They would do this in the autumn because the trees are dryer from the hot summer so they are easier to cut as well as easier to burn. If you wait until the winter months, the trees are frozen and are too moist to light on fire.

Being from the city and never experiencing what a real winter is, we had zero knowledge of this. So obviously we didn't prepare and get firewood during the fall and when we got our first really cold day, we had no way of heating the house. It was in early December and the day started out cold enough to have the ground frozen. Lee and Richard decided it would be good to build a fire to keep the house warm. At first they went out around our yard and tried to gather some branches on the ground, but like I said, they were frozen and too wet to burn. Remember what I said that whenever Lee and Richard would try some dumb stuff to do, it was usually when mom wasn't at home. Well, even though we moved out of San Jose and our address changed, the dumbass stuff traveled with us.

Mom made this pretty cool design in our front yard to separate our driveway from the front yard. To make this design, mom used railroad ties that we found at the backside of our property. Mom was always industrious and knew how to use anything to be creative.

Lee and Richard must have already been seriously high because for whatever reason they thought about using the railroad ties to make the fire. The railroad ties were wood, had an oily surface so hey, it should be easy to burn. They go outside and pick up a railroad tie, place it in the chimney. Naturally it lit easy and at first it started out really warm. Then about 10 minutes later this plume of black smoke starts to puff out from inside our chimney and into our living room.

I'm sure that Lee and Richard then realized that yes railroad ties would be easy to catch on fire and yes, they would burn. But they also got a lesson in chemistry because when lacquer oil, tar and wood is on fire it creates this highly toxic gas that if you inhale enough, it can kill you. Not only does it create toxic fumes, but once it is lit, it becomes very difficult to extinguish because water and oil don't really mix.

So now the house is completely filled with toxic black smoke and we all have to get outside. By now Rhonda comes running up from down the road because she thinks our house is on fire. Well, in a way it kind of is. Lee and Richard still need to figure out how to extinguish the fire and get the railroad tie out of the chimney.

At least now they thought of a smart idea. They went and got the wheelbarrow and blankets. They soaked the blankets in water and used the blankets to grab the railroad tie and throw it into the wheelbarrow. They then took the smoldering block of wood tar outside and threw it onto the cold frozen ground far from our house.

Now they have to air out the house so they run around the house and open every door and window. We still had to wait and couldn't go back inside so we had to stand on frozen ground outside in the bitter cold. After an hour or so the house finally airs out so we can finally go back inside.

When we walk back in, all we can see is black soot on everything from the floor to the ceiling. We are still cold but before we can close up the windows and doors, we need to wipe down the soot and clean the entire house. I guess the one good thing about this entire fiasco was it did happen during the day so we still had time to figure out how to keep warm because it gets really cold at night.

Instead of asking Rhonda or the other neighbor down the road for some pieces of wood, these two boneheads came up with an even more brilliant idea than the railroad ties. Inside of our house we had plenty of dry wood that we could use to create a fire and burn safely in our chimney. So, as you are reading this part of my story, if you were to look around your house, what kind of items do you think you could use to make a fire?

Yes...that's right. Dumbass one and Dumbass two got the axe and started to chop up our dining room table and chairs, the coffee table and bookshelf. To their credit, it worked and kept our house home for the night. But I guess we'll figure out where to sit down and eat later.

Later that evening mom gets home and it didn't take mom long to realize something had happened in her house. Even though we tried to clean the best we could, nobody ever cleaned the way mom did. She could still see the smudges on the walls and ceilings and the soot dust on the couches (at least Lee and Richard didn't chop these up to burn). But the biggest clue for mom was when she would get home, she would always walk into the kitchen and place her purse on the table. Mom was really smart but even an idiot could have figured out the table and chairs were missing. She looked at Lee and Richard and in her typical mom voice said, "What the hell happened?"

Beavis and Butthead tell mom the story and even though she couldn't sit down and drink her coffee she did find the humor in the story. She looked around, shrugged her shoulders and said, "Well, at least you didn't blow up my microwave again."

Mom always had a way of looking at the bright-side of things. The whole time I hear them tell mom the story, I can't help but to think, why didn't they at least try to burn mom's trusty weapon… "The Board." But no, that damn thing still hung above our refrigerator.

# Chapter 20
## Dumbasses …Farmers

I wish I could say that the shenanigans and goofiness ended because we moved, but actually now that they saw the cousins more often the stupid experiments just grew. For one thing, they never ran out of pot to smoke because they found out that being on a vast farm in the middle of nowhere you could actually grow your own marijuana without getting caught.

Now if they had an entrepreneur mindset, they could have made some money, albeit illegally but at least they wouldn't have to hustle around looking for odd jobs. But not these guys. You may have heard this saying, "Never get high on your own supply." Well, I guess my brothers and cousins had a different motto "We're always high because we grow our own supply." They would even plan ahead for the winter months and grow enough to store up ahead of time.

They even figured out how to grow pot inside the house. They would have to be sneaky so mom couldn't find out so they would use their closets. They would line the closets with aluminum foil and hang a grow lamp and then plant the seeds in 5 gallon buckets. Like I said, if these guys would ever put their brains to good use, they probably would have made millions of dollars.

Lee and Bill were the brains of the operation. Lee grew his pot at our house and Bill grew at Aunty Louise's house. Raymond was just the go along guy but Ronald and Richard were the sneaky guys Lee and Bill would have to watch out for. If Richard and Ronald could, they would have been high like 32 hours of every day. Yes, I know there are only 24 hours in a day, but I just wanted to emphasize that these two loved to spend the entire day flying as high as they could. So, when Lee and Bill would store up the pot to get them through the winter months, they couldn't tell Ronald or Richard because they would sneak some and smoke as much as they could.

So as Lee would harvest the plants, he would have to hide the stash. Every day Lee would come home and the first thing he would do would go check his stash. This one day he comes home and he can't find it. He immediately knows who to find...Richard and Ronald. But the guys are nowhere to be found.

A day goes by and the thinking is that the guys may have found girls and were just out partying. Then another day goes by and now Lee, Bill and Raymond start to look all over our property. Lee and Richard had built forts all over the place so they spent the day searching everywhere.

Now the third day comes and Richard and Ronald still have not been found so now my mom is starting to get a little concerned. Later on that day, mom is getting dressed and she happens to look down and see an extension cord going into her closet. She follows the cord and notices that it disappears underneath the crawl space in her closet floor. We would hear mom tell grandma and Aunty Louis the story "I'm getting dressed and I look down at the floor and I notice a cord going into the crawl space door. I'm thinking to myself, no way. Are these dumb asses really underneath the house?" She tells Lee and Bill to come into the room and open up the crawl space. Sure enough. Richard and Ronald were underneath the house.

Why do you ask? They had found Lee's pot stash and instead of taking some and going to smoke outside, they took it all and hid underneath the house. They had set up a lamp, had blankets, food and water. I guess when nobody was around, they would come up and sneak more food or use the restroom.

So, mom looks down at them, shakes her head and says, "Get your asses out of there."

From the pot standpoint, at least they did have Bill's supply, but needless to say…Lee had to find a better hiding place.

# Chapter 21
## Starting School…The New Kid

The school we went to was two small buildings that had all the grades from Kindergarten to 12th grade. One building was for the elementary students and the next building was for all the upper grades. It was somewhat cool because at least I got to see my sister sometimes. But for the most part it was a sucky school. The playground was only dirt with monkey bars and a goofy climbing structure that was more for 3 or 4 year olds than bigger kids.

The school was far away from our house so we couldn't walk to it like I did before. Instead, we had to wake up at 6 am in the morning to get ready for the bus to pick us up at 6:30. Our school day didn't start until 8:00 am so we had to sit on the bus for like an hour. The roads were all dirt so if you sat in the back of the bus, you bounced around so high you'd almost hit your head on the roof. All the kids for the school rode the bus, so even though this was all new to me, at least I had my big sister to ride with.

One thing that was cool was I was now able to play sports for the school. Even though it was a small school, they had team sports that would play against other small schools. I played for the basketball team and the baseball team. There weren't enough players to make a football team but we still played at lunch time.

At least my blazing speed traveled with me so anytime I got to show off I would. This made me popular with the other kids and none of the guys wanted to race me.

When we moved, I was in the 4th grade and being the new kid was a new experience for me. I made a few friends, I remember Vance, Ronny, Zack and Justin. We played every day while at school, but unlike Buckner, we never saw each other after school because none of us lived close by. That was another adjustment so all my playing had to be done during recess or lunch times.

Since I wasn't able to play with anyone after school or on the weekends, I did what any kid my age would do, I made a lot of imaginary friends. I had a vivid imagination and it was great because usually I'd score all the touchdowns or make all the baskets. But sometimes it sucked because my imaginary friends were so real to me that trying to play Butts Up or Hide and Go Seek was difficult. I did try, but my imaginary friends had trouble catching the ball and I never could find them when they hid.

Even though I didn't have any neighborhood friends, except that girl, at least I still had my "other" friends. I still loved playing football so when I got home, I'd play a game. I would grab my football, toss it high up in the air, run and go catch it and then start running and juking out my friends. I had a seriously good imagination because I still don't know how they tackled me.

## PUBERTY

By the time 6th grade started I hit the dreaded puberty stage. The girls that seemed to annoy me, now looked different to me. When school started that year, Marcia and Becky came back and something happened to them. All the sudden they didn't look like just girls, they morphed into a whole different creature. They had boobies. That 6th grade year I spent more time at lunch and recess hanging with them then with my friends.

One fond memory I have from my schooling years was with Becky. Holding hands was a big thing in 6th grade but the whole goal was to get to first base. If you could kiss a girl, you would get the ultimate street cred and respect. You had done something that all the other guys were too afraid to even try. Becky was my girl so we held hands as we walked around the playground. This was cool and made everyone else jealous. My hand wasn't scratching my butt or picking my nose like the other guys because I was actually holding a girl's hand. My other buddy was Justin and his girl was Marcia. The four of us together were like power couples. Even the upperclassmen took notice of us.

We've been holding hands almost the whole year and now the end of the school year is getting close. The question started to come around...are either of us going to be able to get a kiss before summer break? Up to this point, me and Justin were the envy of all the guys. Not only did we get to hold our girlfriends' hands, we had the two hottest girls. But now, the guys started to tease us.

"You can't kiss her…you can't kiss her," we'd hear them chant as we strolled through the playground.

Of course, girls being girls, Marcia and Becky just smiled and didn't say anything.

Are the girls wanting to kiss us? Man, that would have been a huge risk to try. What would happen if we did try and they rejected us, or even slapped us? Or even worse, what if we didn't know what to do and our very first kiss was horrible and they laughed at us? The pressure of a first kiss is beyond stressful, it's downright frightful. Talk about being nervous…and now we are getting called out by all the other guys. We had no idea what we should do.

So, Justin and I made a pack that we were going to try and plant a kiss on our girl. But with us being guys, competition now set in. Who was going to be the first and if one got the kiss would the other one be able to get one as well? By this time word was out and I'm sure that Becky and Marcia are well aware of the dilemma we are in. But again, they just smiled and never said a word.

The spring concert was coming up and the older classes would be putting on a performance. The concert would be like 2 weeks before the end of the school year. If there was ever going to be a time to close the deal and plant a kiss it was going to be at the concert. So, all four of us are holding hands while we walk into the gym and we sit next to each other. I think the entire school knew what was about to go down.

For some reason I developed this incredible amount of courage. I'm holding Becky's hand with my left hand and I turn, look her in the eyes and plant one right on the lips. Success!!! I did it. I kissed a girl. Only shortly after I finished my quest, Justin and Marcia started to kiss. And man, they are really kissing!!! I thought the peck I did was awesome, but here these two are in full open mouth and closed eye make out session. I'm just in awe of what is going on right next to me.

All the kids in the auditorium just start oohing and awing and when they stop, they even get a round of applause. Even the upperclassmen were impressed. Justin seriously up staged me. Could I do that? No way, I didn't have enough practice time on my pillow to pull that off. So, Becky and I sit there still holding hands and I guess ok with our kiss. But for Justin and Marcia, the last couple weeks of the school year they became the "real" power couple. But I thought, I'm going to spend the whole summer practicing because when we start back next school year, me and Becky are going to make out in front of the whole school on the first day and I'm going to get my power couple reputation back.

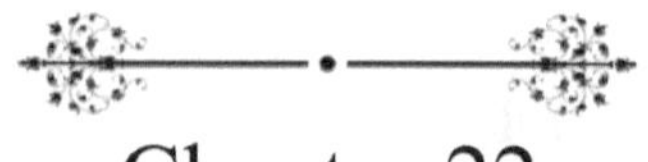

# Chapter 22
## Dutch's Bar

When we lived on Buckner Drive, mom worked as an engineer as an assembly worker. She did her job but as I would later learn she referred to it as a "number job." What she meant was she was more of a number and not a person and anyone of the employees could easily be replaced.

Mom tried to find jobs around Niangua or in the surrounding small towns, but jobs were really hard to come by. So, mom found a job at Dutch's Bar about 40 minutes away. She would leave the house after we got home from school at 3 pm and she would work from 4 pm to closing time at 2 am.

Mom actually enjoyed working at Dutch's. She enjoyed being around people but I would soon learn that working at a bar fit mom's personality. She was a no-nonsense person and if she could have, she would have brought her board with her to work. But instead of needing "The Board" mom was always equipped with her cold eyed Clint Eastwood stare. People in the bar knew mom meant business and like at our house, she ran the bar. If people drank too much, she cut them off and if they complained she kicked them out and if they didn't leave peacefully, she banned them for a week. Just like on Buckner, mom didn't play and just with all of us kids, the patrons at Dutch's Bar would soon learn that as well. This little petite woman would stare down a 6'5" 300lb grown man and bring him to his knees. Mom gained so much respect from the owner would give her the keys to the building and entrust her to run the place.

## REAL PEOPLE

Like many child-parent relationships, the older the child gets the more the parent-child relationship evolves to being a mentor, advisor and friend. When I started to get older mom and I would just start talking. I would soon understand why mom needed to move to Missouri and why she loved working at the bar. I was in my early 20s and this one time while sitting at the table me, mom and Kerry and started one of our many talks. By this time, I had already gone through the teenage craziness and the three of us were just enjoying our chat.

The one thing about mom, is nothing was off the table. We could talk about anything. For some reason our discussion turned to Buckner and what happened. Mom told us the "Real" story and we began to understand. Mom said that she and dad actually tried to work it out, but after a few months she just realized things could never be the same. And to our surprise, things were very different than what me and Kerry thought. We were just kids so we only saw things through a kid's eyes instead of what was reality.

Mom said she just got tired of being surrounded by fakeness. She said that we were the "Brady Bunch" outside but on the inside of the house she and dad were not close at all. Dad spent so much time at work and any free time he had he would either be golfing, bowling or fishing. Come to think about it, Kerry and I talked and we tried to think of our memories of dad as well. We have very fond memories of mom, but when it came to dad, aside from the obvious "Door" story, we had very little recollection of dad being involved with us growing up outside of coaching our teams.

Mom went on to share that the reason she enjoyed working at Dutch's is because she felt like for the first time she was around real people and could just be herself. She didn't have to put on airs about being the perfect wife or mom. She could just be Joyce. Even though people that attended the bar drank, for the most part it was just a group of people coming together, socializing and treating each other with respect. You had farmers, construction workers, teachers and even people who worked in law enforcement. It didn't matter if you were married, divorced, had 10 kids or no kids. Once you came into Dutch's bar, you were part of the family.


## THE ACCIDENT

It was a cold night in February 1984 and mom was driving home from work. Sometime around 3 am she hit a patch of ice and drifted off the road and down a steep ditch. The car would hit a fence pole and make mom's car flip over. Mom wasn't wearing a seatbelt which just so happened to be a blessing, because if she was wearing her seatbelt the crash would have killed her because the car rolled down the hill completely destroying the car. Instead, mom would get thrown from the car and hit a tree about 20 feet up from the ground. She then fell breaking several branches on the way down landing on the cold frozen ground and waited for help. Thank God a person just so happened to be traveling at that same early morning and saw the accident. The driver rushed to the closest house and called 911. An ambulance came and was able to rush mom to the hospital with-in the hour with Kerry riding with her.

Mom hit the tree on her left side and she broke her arm, ribs and thigh bone. As she slid down the tree her leg would get gashed and literally torn away from her knee to her hip. Mom would stay in the hospital for 3 months and would need a steel rod inserted as well as have 19 surgeries to reconstruct her leg. She would also have to endure several months of physical therapy to regain enough strength to walk on her own again. In looking at the results of the crash, with or without her wearing the seatbelt, the sheriffs said there is no way she should have survived the accident because they had never seen anything like it.

This was another very interesting time for our family, not only did we have the life changing experience of the accident, my sister was actually in the same hospital giving birth to her first child.

You would think mom would be disappointed with Kerry getting pregnant while still in high school, but that wasn't mom. Mom's motto was life is hard so you just have to keep pressing forward. So even with Kerry having a child so young or that this horrific accident happened, mom's spirit would not be broken. After several months when mom was finally able to start walking on her own, she wanted to go back to work.

The accident was not going to stop her from living. And not just that, now that she was a grandma, she was going to embrace that head on as well.

When she arrived back on her first day, Dutch's bar was filled from wall to wall. Me, Lee, Richard and Kerry were all with her for this moment. And there was mom standing in her second home, holding her new grandbaby and getting greeted by her other family. Mom's second family was there to embrace and welcome her back with open arms. I think she needed Dutch's bar as much as Dutch's bar needed her.

# Chapter 23
## Springfield…Dumbass Genetics

L ife would change again after the accident. Because mom required multiple physical therapy sessions and checkups, we had to move to the city to be closer to the hospital. We moved to Springfield Missouri. After living in the middle of nowhere, now I was at least surrounded by actual houses, sidewalks and neighbors. I even had friends that lived on the same street. The move to Niangua affected me negatively but the move to Springfield helped me because I actually developed really good friendships…not imaginary.

Our family seemed to be nomadic, because when we moved, so did Grandma, Aunty Louise and the cousins. Richard and Lee were much older so Richard bought his own house and Lee lived with me, Kerry (her baby) and mom.

When we lived on Buckner Drive, our house was the hub for all the neighborhood kids and in Niangua it was the hub for my cousins, brothers, sister and her friends. Because mom always focused on creating a welcoming environment, when we lived in Springfield, our home on Pierce Street became the hub for me and my friends.

Similar to my brothers and their friends, I had a group of friends that all lived a few houses down from me. Cole lived at one corner and Gerald lived at the other. Johnny lived around the corner so pretty much every day we were always together. It must be a teenage boy thing during the 80's because just like my older brothers, goofy stuff would usually occur when we were together. It didn't matter what time of year or day it was, we generally found any adventure to do that usually involved getting into trouble.

You think that my brothers would want to give me some advice and wisdom about making good decisions, but no. Instead, they just laughed and even encouraged us more. It was so bad that when we would go around stealing stuff, my brothers or cousins would buy it from us. They would even give us items to look for.

Like this one time, Richard wanted a riding lawn mower. So late one night we searched the neighborhood and snuck into garages and found the perfect riding lawn mower to steal. We sneak into the garage and push the lawn mower out to the street and down to the end of the block. Once we get far enough away I jump onto the lawn mower and start it up.

If you've never heard a riding lawn mower engine, it gets really loud. So here we are like 3am in the morning in dead silence and you hear this roaring lawn mower engine. Honestly the sound didn't really bother us, it was the fact that we could only drive like 5mph. This thing is so loud and we are barely even moving then we start to see porch lights turning on. It's not like we would have any good reason to explain why we are driving a lawn mower on the street in the wee hours of the morning, so we have to turn it off.

My brother only lived a couple of blocks from us so we just pushed it all the way to his house. It took us like 2 hours to only go a couple blocks and afterwards my brother would give us 5.00 each. Was it really worth it? From the money standpoint, no, but from the adventure and thrilling stand point...absolutely.

## TRAIN HOPPING

I guess we learned a few tricks from my brother Richard because whenever we came up with an idea, we acted with impulse and didn't think of potential for pain or consequences. Instead, we just thought let's do it, what could possibly go wrong? Not too far from us were train tracks. From time to time, we would go there to party. We would have to go to the local 7 Eleven and try to pay someone who was old enough to buy us some beer. So, it's late one warm summer night and we head to 7-Eleven, successfully get some beer, and we go to the train tracks.

Word must have gotten out because by the time we got to our spot, there were like a dozen other people there, including girls. We've brought the beer so naturally we are already the cool dudes. We're hanging out drinking beer and watching the trains go by. You think this would be boring, but anytime we could get beer and have girls nearby it was anything but boring.

This train comes by and it's not going too fast. Gerald all the sudden jumps up and decides to run after the train. He grabs the side rails and pulls himself up off the ground. He rides down a few yards, jumps off and comes running back. That was freaking AWESOME!!! So now, me, Johnny and Cole all join in. As the train cars go by, we start running beside it, grab the bars and ride along for a few yards. It was also cool when we would jump off because we would generally land on our feet and roll over like stunt men.

Everyone was envious of us. The other guys were too afraid and the girls just looked at us like we were totally the hottest guys there. So naturally we have to take up another level. Another train comes by and we start the process over again. But now I want to be even more daring. Instead of just holding on to the railing I decided to climb up the ladder to the top of the train car. I got all the way up and now I'm standing on top of a moving train. Johnny, Gerald and Cole soon follow. We have gone to a whole other level.

Everyone is cheering us on and we actually start jumping from one boxcar to the next boxcar. Even though it was about a 5 foot gap between the boxcars, the train wasn't going too fast so it wasn't as hard as you would think. After a few successful leaps we get to this one boxcar and we are standing on top getting ready to jump. We didn't notice that the boxcar we were about to jump to was filled with logs. Me being me and thinking like Richard, decided to just jump first. So, I leap and land on a log but then the log rolls and I lose my footing. I actually fall to the side and I'm able to catch myself with one hand. Here I am, halfway off the top of a traveling train car and holding on by one hand. Thankfully my best buds made the jump safely and came running to me. Johnny grabs me by my shoulders, Gerald and Cole grab my legs and they all pull me back into the boxcar.

We finally decided that we had enough fun for the time, so we carefully climbed back down the train car and jumped off. We were now rock stars and could have our pick of any of the girls but for some reason I wasn't feeling cool enough. Instead, I felt like I needed to change my pants.

## GRANDMA'S LITTLE RED CAR

Sometimes stories just seem to repeat themselves. As we went through middle school the bolder, or rather dumber, things we would do. It was the summer of my 8th grade year and just like on Buckner, anytime something happened it would be during the day when mom was not around. Mom and grandma were helping a friend out during the day so I had the house to myself.

By this time, the four of us were all about girls and usually when we had them on our mind, we lost our ability to think. During the day, if we weren't outside doing something, we were usually inside talking on the phone to girls. Gerald had this girlfriend named Stephanie that lived on the other side of town. So, on this day, Gerald was talking to his girlfriend and Stephanie just so happened to have 3 of her friends over at her house. Well, me, Johnny and Cole are Gerald's three friends so of course we want to go over.

Even though we've ridden our bikes everywhere around Springfield, Stephanie lived further than we've gone before so it would have taken us all day to get there. So now that we have our hormones in full effect, we need to think of a better way to get there. I look over on the counter and I see my grandma's keys to her little red car. I'm only 14 years old and unfortunately, I haven't really gone through a growth spurt, so I'm still the same size when I was in the 6th grade.

I looked at my buds and came up with the best idea. Mom and grandma aren't going to be home for a long time so let's just take grandma's car and go to Stephanie's house. Of course, Johnny, Cole and Gerald think this is an awesome idea. I grab the keys and we all pile into the little red car. As I mentioned, I haven't gone through my growth spurt so I can't reach the gas or brake pedals. I move the seat all the way up but now I can't really see over the steering wheel.

Just like Richard and Ronald would never be deterred, me and my buddies would not be as well, especially when we had girls to go see. So, Johnny thinks quickly and runs inside the house and comes out carrying phone books. Yes…phone books. And not just one, but two. All three of the guys are taller than me but instead of them driving, they just wanted to make me taller. So now here I am with the seat pushed all the way up, sitting on two phone books and barely able to look over the steering wheel. But hey…at least now it's safe for me to drive.

I start the car and back out of the driveway and off we go. Grandma's car is small so it was easy to control. To avoid the cops, we decide to take the back streets all the way to Stephanie's house. We arrive safely, jump out and now it's time to hang out with Stephanie and all her friends. We got to the front door and Stephanie's older sister answered (who was waaaayyyyy hot) and she told us Stephanie and her friends left. For some reason, boneheaded Gerald forgot to tell Stephanie we were coming over. We didn't have a way to call them so now we decide to just drive around and look for them. We had a car so what was the rush, even if we can't find them, at least we're out on another cool adventure.

We drove around their neighborhood a little while

but then we decided to head to our side of town and show off to our other friends. After a few hours of joyriding, we decided we needed to make it back before mom and Grandma returned home. We pulled in our driveway and put the keys back on the table where we found them. Success…no way would they find out.

But for some reason, we didn't take into consideration that when we drove around showing off to our friends, maybe the neighbors noticed who was driving the car. So later that night, mom would get a call from one of them and the jig was up. Not only that, but it was kind of hard to explain how grandma's car was almost empty on gas. By this time, I guess I outgrew the board, either that or mom felt she needed a much harsher form of punishment. The next day I found myself on the way to Juvenile Hall. I had to spend the next 4 weekends working community service with the other juvenile delinquents..

I guess the moral of the story would be that perhaps it would have been better to break into a golf course and go joy riding. However, given our inability to think, we probably would have left our wallets as well.

## THE "LEMON"

I guess there was something about cars that would add to our sense of adventure and more stupidity. When I turned 16, mom had bought me a bright yellow 72 Chevy Nova. As a kid who was all about image, this car was a piece of crap and I didn't want to have any girls see me driving it. But as a bonehead surrounded by bonehead friends, this was a new awesome toy.

Instead of having to ride our bikes around to act like morons, we had a car that would only help our cause.

The "Lemon," as we would call it, was great to try new things. Usually, the new things revolved around speed. The Lemon only had a 6 cylinder so it wasn't too fast, but we did everything we could to press the limits of what that car could do.

Springfield was a train depot so there were several train tracks around town. We were big on Dukes of Hazzard growing up, obviously because of Daisy Duke but also because the way Bo and Luke Duke would drive around speeding and jumping all over town. This one day while driving around we came to a train track crossing. The crossing had a hill so it was really inviting for us to try the ultimate Dukes of Hazzard experience and see if we could jump it.

As usual all four of us are in the car and then Johnny says, "Punch it."

Naturally I listen to him so I step on the gas and push it to the floor. The tracks were about a block away so we were picking up a good amount of speed. The train tracks had a mound so it created a natural ramp to see if indeed we could jump it. I'm gripping the steering wheel tight and the car is vibrating and shaking. I look down at the speedometer and we're going over 70 mph by the time we get to the tracks. We hit the tracks and actually get air. I'm not wearing a seatbelt and my butt comes off the seat and now we start to fly down the other side. We must have flown 10 feet and the Lemon landed with a loud THUMP and I quickly pressed on the brakes and we skidded about another 10 feet.

We've had this car for a few months by now and since it was a piece of crap, I never bothered to clean it. So, when we landed with the thud every piece of dust and dirt filled inside the car. There was so much dirt that we couldn't even see. All four of us jump out in celebration because we just did the most awesome thing ever. We look at each other and just start laughing, we are covered from head to toe in dirt and it looks like someone just poured a bag of dirty flour all over us. The only unfortunate thing that occurred was we were all yelling, "YEE HAW," so when we landed the dirt and dust got in our mouths so our teeth are grimy and our lips are all black.

The Lemon wasn't exactly built for doing stunts and jumping so when we landed the muffler broke off and was dragging behind the car. There's nothing we could really do about it so we decide to drive home with the muffler sparking behind us. We pull into the driveway and mom is gardening in the front yard. She stares at us with the typical "what the hell did you just do" look. We get out of the car and Gerald comes up with a good lie and says we ran over something so we tried to fix the muffler which is why we were so dirty.

Mom stands knowing we are lying and tilting her head just asks, "So why does it look like you got shit in your mouth?"

We really didn't have a good answer for that one but who cared, we were awesome and built on our legendary status in the neighborhood. We were the Dukes of Hazzard, or rather in mom's view the Dopes of Springfield.

## THE GRAVEYARD

As if jumping and flying through the air wasn't enough adventure, racing was even better. Any time we got a chance to drive fast we did. This one night we are on the way back from a party. We get to a long straight away near the Green Lawn cemetery graveyard. By now no-one needs to say anything, it was just a natural instinct to punch it and press the pedal to the metal. By this time, I should note that it was raining.

I have the gas pressed to the floor and we start picking up speed. We're going as fast as we can and then all the sudden, I hear, "TONY CORNER!!!!!"

I try to slam on the brakes and make the turn, but I'm too late. I get the car sideways and we start to slide off the road and into the grass. The cemetery is surrounded by 4 ft concrete pillars about 10 feet from the road. They probably have these to prevent dumbass people like us from crashing into the graveyard.

Here we are totally out of control and hopelessly sliding around the corner on wet pavement. We slide off the road, down the embankment and plow into one of the poles and just keep sliding on the wet grass. We crashed and slid like 30 feet into the graveyard before we finally stopped.

It's pouring rain and we all jump out of the car to see what the damage is. Johnny was usually in the front seat with me so when he got out, he started laughing and pointing to his door. When I hit the concrete pillar, we got a huge dent in the door. Then we hear Cole and Gerald laughing because they looked down and noticed we literally stopped on someone's grave. Even though it was creepy it was still funny but most of all, we had to get out of there before someone sees us and calls the cops.

Unfortunately, when we hit the concrete pillar, it slid with us and got wedged underneath the car. I put the car in reverse and the guys try to push but we can't move. They run around to the back of the car, I put it in drive and punch it. I was able to get the wheels on the grass in full throttle and get enough traction to get off the concrete pillar. The back tires were spinning and when I was finally able to pull forward the guys were still standing behind the car and mud was flying everywhere. I stopped the car and they jumped back in and we're finally able to get the heck out of the graveyard.

We get back on the road and drive down a ways until we notice the coast is clear. We pull over and we all jump out to have a real celebration. Even though the guys were covered in mud and we crashed into a concrete pillar, put a huge dent in the side door and landed on someone's gravestone it was freaking awesome!!! And honestly, if we could. I know we probably would do it again.

This would be how Johnny would describe it: "I was sitting in the front seat and the road was shining from the rain so it was hard to see too far ahead. Tony is full throttle and we are flying down the road. All the sudden I see the reflection from the arrow sign and I yell, 'Turn.' We are going way too fast and Tony slams on the brakes and tries to turn. The car pitches sideways and we just slide right off the road and smash through a concrete pillar. It was crazy because the car got stuck on the pillar and we had to push it off. When we finally got the car back on the road we couldn't stop laughing. The graveyard never replaced the pillar so even today you can see where we crashed."

I obviously can't hide the smashed in door so in the morning I tell mom that I made a slight dent in the passenger door. Mom goes outside and looks at the door. "Slight my ass, you smashed the door."

Guess mom thought it was best to get rid of my play toy because later that day, mom's friend came and picked up the car and my Lemon was now gone.

## THE MOONSHINES

Now that my Lemon is gone, we needed to have another way to drive around and goof off. Good thing that Johnny's mom would let him drive her car. One day everyone piled into the car and we had other friends and younger brothers in the car so there were like 8 guys stuffed into his car.

Johnny is driving and Me and Gerald are in the backseat sitting behind him. We pull up to the stop light and there is an older grandma and grandpa next to us. I'm not sure who inspired mooning people, but for some reason, a rite of passage for teenage boys is driving around with our naked asses hanging out the windows. So, all the sudden Gerald jumps up, pulls down his shorts and sticks his big fat ass out the window right at them. Johnny drives off and we are all busting up laughing. Well of course this just inspires the rest of us so now anytime we pulled up in a car or it would pass by us we'd all jump up and drop our drawers.

Unfortunately, we are doing this in our neighborhood so it's not like people didn't recognize Johnny driving and it wouldn't have been hard to figure out who the other dumbasses were in the car with him. Johnny turns the corner and we see a car coming towards us. Boom the rest of us jump up, drop our drawers and put our asses out the windows. As we get closer Johnny yells out, "Tony, it's your mom."

I pull my ass out of the window and jump up front into the passenger seat but it's too late and mom passes us.

Johnny sees mom turn around and head back towards us. Johnny pulls over and mom drives up beside us. She yells out, "Tony Lombardi, I know that was you."

I told mom I was up in the front seat, it wasn't me.

Then mom says, "You damn right I know it was you, I know your ass."

I guess I couldn't deny that, she was my mom and has seen my naked butt before. She then says, "Stop being an idiot and get your ass home."

The lesson we learned that day was anytime we decided to go mooning, we made sure to be on the other side of town before putting our asses out the windows.

## PRANKS

My buddies and I would like to pull pranks on neighbors. Basically, dumb stuff like egging houses, toilet papering trees or cars and lighting stink bombs outside their front doors and windows. We were really creative because one night we decided to take the bikes that we would find in our neighbors' yards and climb up trees and hang them from branches. The next morning, we woke up and we saw like 5 or 6 of our neighbors trying to get the bikes down from their trees. Unfortunately like my brothers, we would soon garner the reputation of trouble makers.

On a particular night in the summer, we were feeling exceptionally stupid with fireworks...again how crazy I caught the dumbass genetics. There was an older lady that lived across the street from us and she was the neighbor that would tattle tale to my mom anytime I was doing stuff. It was about midnight so everything was quiet and we filled up my duffle bag and snuck over to her front yard. Then we all grabbed our arsenal and started to shoot off bottle rockets, roman candles and M80's and just ambush the poor old lady's house. It was crazy loud. We blasted her home for like 5 minutes before we started to notice porch lights turning on from the other neighbors. So, we run back home and celebrate our awesome ambush attack but before we go inside my house, I have to hide the evidence so I find a good spot.

The next morning my mom wakes me up in bed. She asks, what did you do? I'm a 15 year old teenage boy, so what was my obvious answer "nothing." Mom then said, well I think you need to come to the front door and tell the Sheriffs that. What do I have to hide, no way am I going to get caught. I go to the front door and there standing with my duffle bag still filled with leftover fireworks are 2 Sheriff Deputies.

I'm still trying to get out of being caught so I said, "That's not my bag."

Mom looked at me with a beyond pissed off look and said, "That's his bag, and you better go get the other 3 boys."

Now 2 more Sheriff car's show up and go pick up Johnny, Gerald and Cole and bring them to my house. Here we are all four of us with 4 Sheriff Deputies in my living room and we are still laughing and making jokes.

The problem was we didn't just cause mischief or vandalize. Because we were stupid enough to not just light up fireworks, we shot them at the old lady's house. They were talking to my mom about assault and destruction of property. These were actual things you could be arrested for.

All four of us are sitting there and now we're starting to freak out…are we really going to go to jail? As the Sheriffs are talking to mom, I'm thinking she will take care of it and ground me and take away my bike for a week or something like that. Mom still has the Clint Eastwood look and she turned to all of us with a cold stare and simply said, "Take them away."

Wow…we must have screwed up seriously. The Deputies walked over to us, put us in handcuffs, took us outside and put us each in a cop car.

Naturally cop cars brought attention to our house so by this time, the whole neighborhood was out front watching this. I'm sure most of the neighbors were thinking it was about time. But with all the other kids, our reputation of being rebels just grew. We really are the bad boys. But now, as tough as we may think we are, we are on our way to jail. This is a Friday morning and all of this happens before noon.

We get to the County Jail and the Deputies walk us inside and put us into the holding cell. All four of us are sitting there in a big box surrounded by bars with our hands still cuffed behind our backs. We are the only ones there, but at least we are still together. One by one they start to take us out. Johnny was first, they walked him up to the counter, took his finger prints and pictures. After they do this, they then take him through a metal door and we don't see him again. Then they came for Cole and Gerald was after that and I was the last one sitting, by myself with no one around.

They finally come to get me and do the same process. After the pictures they take me through the metal door and start to take me down the hallway. The hallway is surrounded by doors but you can't see anyone in there. I'm a little guy but still had 2 big Deputies holding my arms walking beside me. They walk me down to an open door, put me inside and then slam the door behind me. Holy crap!!! I really am arrested.

I'm looking inside a metal box that is like the size of my closet, with a metal toilet and a plastic mat for a bed that has a nasty ass wool blanket that I'm sure is filled with every disease possible. I just stood there in silence. What just happened? Just a few hours earlier I was dreaming about Debbie Gibson and now I'm standing in a cold jail cell.

Pretty soon I hear Johnny yelling, "Tony" and I yell back "Johnny." Then dumbass Gerald yells, "Let's break out of here." (like that was even possible).

We can't see each other but at least we could hear each other. We are yelling back and forth and Gerald is telling us his escape plans and then we hear a deputy yell, "Shut the Hell Up!!!"

Think it was time for us to stop yelling.

After what seemed like hours, I soon heard my name called again… "Tony, I'm getting out of here" yells Johnny.

I guess his dad posted his bail and he was getting released. I'm yelling at him to not forget about me. Soon after I hear the same thing for Cole and

Gerald…now I'm getting concerned and tell them they better come back to get me out. At this time, I'm not even sure if my mom was going to bail me out.

Getting arrested was bad enough but it was a Friday and I was supposed to pick up my girlfriend at 7 pm. We had been dating for months and her parents finally allowed me to take her out. Up to this point, I was only able to go to her house while her parents were home to spend time with her. Even though I did sneak over a few times, for her parents to allow her to spend time alone outside of their view was a big deal. As you can imagine I didn't really have a good reputation so her parents didn't really approve of me. I seriously considered making her my one phone call but no way could I come up with a good excuse outside of the obvious.

So, I'm sitting in my cell for what seems like hours because and the whole time I'm thinking that no way am I going to make the date and for sure her parents will never allow her to see me again. Not only am I thinking about not making the date, but this is also a Friday night and I know that pretty soon some grown ass drunk man named "Bubba" will be put in my cell. Now I am really getting nervous.

Finally, I hear, "Lombardi, you made bail."

Thank you…mom came to my rescue. They came and let out and walked me upstairs and there was my mom, staring at me with her cold Clint Eastwood eyes. We walked to the car and she didn't say a word. The whole ride home we just sat there in silence. We pull into the driveway and before we get out of the car, she turns to me and simply says, "That's your one-time, but don't ever let it happen again because next I won't bail your ass out."

I'm finally out of jail and in the safety of my home, but unfortunately it was 9 pm so I missed my date. The first thing I did when I got inside was call my girlfriend. She answers and before I can even say something she asks, "Why did you get arrested?"

I didn't even have a chance to come up with a good lie about why I wasn't there at 7 pm.

By the time I got home word had already spread that the four of us had been arrested and taken to jail. The good thing is she wasn't too mad and covered for me with her parents. To this day I still can't imagine why her parents didn't like me…

I wish I could say that I would get a little wiser, but for some reason, me, Johnny, Gerald and Cole just had way too much fun and adventures. So, by the time I finally graduated (after going to summer school every year), I had to spend a lot of weekends picking up trash for community service. But at least I did avoid getting arrested again.


## REBEL KID


My time in Springfield wasn't easy on my mom. I was a problem child who was acting out. I just wanted to find as many ways to get into as much trouble as possible. I guess I had the same dumbass gene that Lee, Richard and the cousins all had. In looking back, I probably should have spent far more time in jail or at least juvenile hall. Either that or mom should have locked me in my room and grounded me my whole teenage years.

When I finally matured (many years later) I

remember one of our conversations and we talked about our time in Springfield. Mom said those were tough times on all of us. She said she just prayed every day that I didn't do anything to hurt myself or someone else really bad. She also said that I was much more different than Lee or Richard growing up. Usually, she only heard about their stuff later, but for some reason just like when I was a kid trying to hide the Board, she always would catch me.

It's not like half the stuff I did was hard to figure out. Joyriding in Grandma's car, terrorizing the old lady across the street, not being able to hide a huge dent in the car door and yes of course, driving past my mom with my bare ass hanging out the window. I guess in this sense, maybe my brothers were smarter than me, they knew how to hide the evidence or at least come up with better excuses. In retrospect, maybe "I" was really the dumbass brother…

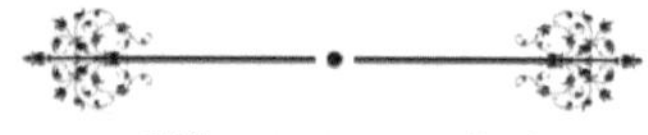

# Chapter 24
## Thicker Than Blood

Soon after graduating High School I would realize that if I didn't leave my surroundings, the path I was on was headed straight for destruction. Even though I loved my friends, I knew that if I didn't make a change, I would wind up being an alcoholic, married and divorced twice with 4 kids by the time I was 25.

I moved back to California but I would come back periodically to visit with family and friends. It was like we were teenagers all over again and always having a great time together. But eventually relationships just drift apart, especially over distance and time. Over the next few years and after my family ultimately moved, my trips would become more infrequent. I really didn't have any reason to visit aside from my friends, which by this time, life really started to take hold in their lives.

Gerald unfortunately got caught up in the party scene and would be in and out of jail. Cole wound up getting married and divorced a couple of times and had multiple kids with each of his wives. Johnny was the only one that stayed on the straight and narrow. He was a hard partier as well but after Gerald started to head down that path, he decided he needed to make a change for the better so he started to distance himself from that life.

Recently I visited Springfield for family matters and I was able to catch up with Johnny. He lost contact with

Cole several years ago and also, at the time of my visit, Gerald was currently locked up in jail. Johnny and I spent lunch together and just talked. Of course, we spent time reminiscing about the old times and how we should have all either been dead, in rehab or in jail with Gerald. But mostly we spent time talking and sharing together as men. We sat for hours and both shared stories about things we have done in our adult lives.

I may not have had the brother experience of growing up with Richard and Lee, but in that moment, I knew I had a brother for life. We don't have to talk every day or even see each other very often to realize that the connection we had will last forever. When you are a teenage boy and all you have are your friends, you develop a relationship and bond that can almost be thicker than blood. From middle school to graduation the four of us were closer than brothers. It's sad sometimes how life happens and seasons just change.

I had to catch my flight in a couple of hours so we walked outside and we gave each other a hug and then Johnny said something that until that time, I didn't realize I needed to hear…he said, "You did the right thing Tony."

I always had in the back of my mind this sense of guilt because I left my best friends behind. I looked at him and my eyes swelled up. We both said we loved each other and hugged one more time. It was as if we knew we most likely won't see each other again and we wanted one last memory of our brotherly love.

Even as I write this chapter it is hard to see the screen through my tears. It's amazing to me how impactful moments in time can be and they will carry you the rest of your life. I look back fondly of the times we had causing mayhem, chasing girls and I also remember them standing by my side as we all carried my brother's casket. Any time I needed them they were there. I just hope that perhaps they feel the same about this time in our life as I do and maybe they too cherish the brotherhood we had.

Now that I am in my 50's, I would love to go back to a brief moment in time when even though things were difficult, life was also simpler. The time before we had life's responsibilities of a job, marriage, children and house payments. I love my life now but I'm sure all of us can close our eyes and think of those moments…the special moments that just bring joy to our hearts and a smile to our face.

My moment would be to have the four of us back together again and get on our bikes for one last midnight ride. We'll be rocking our mullets, 501 jeans, Coke-Cola shirts, converse and pulling wheelies on our Schwinn, Mongoose and DiamondBack bikes. The memories would pour over us like a waterfall and I'd imagine the tears would be streaming down all of our cheeks just the same...

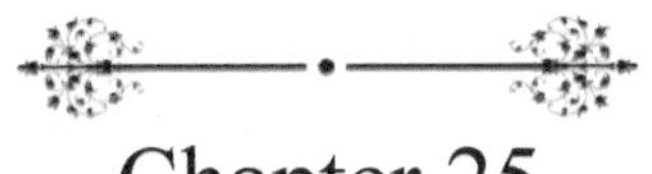

# Chapter 25
## One Last Door

After I graduated high school and moved back to California and my sister would move to Arizona with her child (and soon to be second one) and Grandma moved with her. Lee, Richard and mom still lived in Springfield. Unfortunately, times would continue to get tough and more tragedies would hit our family, most notably my mom.

I can't go into too much detail about the story, but the person who was considered the anchor of our family would develop a sickness and find the need to end his life. It was in the spring of 94' and Lee, mom and her friend were in the house and while in his room, Lee took a rifle and shot himself. Till this day the memory of his funeral still haunts all of us. We all loved him and accepted his decision, but the hurt, pain and void left in all of us will never leave us.

Shortly after Lee died, mom felt it necessary to leave Springfield and once again seek solace from Grandma and Kerry in Arizona. Richard accompanied her as well and of course being the nomads, Aunty Louise and cousins had all migrated there. A few years after living in Arizona, mom would come home from her job (as a bartender) and she would find Richard floating in her pool. Unfortunately, Richard had dove into the pool head first and broke his neck.

It is hard to think of my mom and not think about adversity, strength and perseverance. Throughout my adult life I would spend as much time speaking to my mom on the phone, but mostly I enjoyed any time my sister, mom and I would be able to get together for a chat at the table. Mom was my confidant, my supporter, my advisor and at times, my admonisher. Even though she was much older and more petite, she still carried the wisdom of an owl and always had just the right words that I always needed to hear.

As my adult life continued, mom would always be there to share with me everyday life experiences. When I was blessed to find the love of my life, my mom would be there to listen to my frustrations and advise me on what it means to be a good partner and husband. When I was blessed with my two beautiful children, my mom would listen to my frustrations and advise me on how to be a good leader and father. If there is anyone who I could look at for inspiration about how to deal with life's obstacles it is my mom.

When I would have a funny moment, I could hear mom's great laugh. When I have a sad moment, I would hear mom say, "That's ok honey."

And when things get tough, I can always hear mom saying, "That's life honey, you just have to keep pressing forward." It's amazing the impact our parents (positive or negative) can have on us.

The good, bad and ugly moments are what life is all about and my mom dealt with everything thrown her way. It is strange how life can change in a moment. It took many years of discussion and healing to realize that we just have to embrace the changes in our lives. We never know which door will open for us and more importantly, we never know what is on the other side. As I would learn the strength from my mom that we can't live our life in fear and avoid the doors, but rather we need to embrace the door and just attack whatever life presents us on the other side. We may find the love of our life to marry or we may find the love of our life in bed with another person. In either scenario, it's what we do in that moment that determines our life path.

I'm sure my mom didn't appreciate walking in on my dad. But mom would later tell us that she wouldn't have changed a thing. She embraced the unfortunate event and would use that to change her life in a positive way. In a sense, her life on Buckner died that fateful day but it also began when we moved to Niangua. Like she would say, "Honey when one door closes, another door opens."

Mom always had these tidbits of wisdom to always pass on.

On Christmas of 2018, I took my wife and two children to visit my sister and mom in Arizona. My mom wasn't feeling too well and I thought the best Christmas gift I could give her would be for her to see her grandchildren. It was a great visit and my mom cherished what she called the best Christmas gift she's ever received. I know this because when we flew back my mom would call and leave me that message. I still have the message saved on my phone. This brought tears to my eyes because I feel so proud that I could bring her a little joy and possibly repay a fraction of what she's done for me. Two months later, and with my sister Kerry by her side, mom would decide it was time to go to sleep. She had lived and loved a very full life and she was finally able to no longer "have to press forward." Instead, she was finally able to receive a much deserved rest.

Hopefully I have a long time to wait, but someday I'm looking forward to seeing my mom and running up to her and getting the big momma hug, kiss on the forehead and hear the most beautiful words, "Hi Honey."

To my mom...

www.ingramcontent.com/pod-product-compliance
Lightning Source LLC
Chambersburg PA
CBHW021213130726
47988CB00002B/630